WHY BOYS FAIL

Why Boys Fail

**Saving Our Sons from an Educational
System That's Leaving Them Behind**

Richard Whitmire

Foreword by Michelle Rhee,
Chancellor, District of Columbia Public Schools

AMACOM

AMERICAN MANAGEMENT ASSOCIATION

New York • Atlanta • Brussels • Chicago • Mexico City • San Francisco
Shanghai • Tokyo • Toronto • Washington, D.C.

Special discounts on bulk quantities of AMACOM books are
available to corporations, professional associations, and other
organizations. For details, contact Special Sales Department,
AMACOM, a division of American Management Association,
1601 Broadway, New York, NY 10019.
Tel: 800-250-5308. Fax: 518-891-2372.
E-mail: specialsls@amanet.org
Website: www.amacombooks.org/go/specialsales
To view all AMACOM titles go to: www.amacombooks.org

This publication is designed to provide accurate and authoritative
information in regard to the subject matter covered. It is sold with the
understanding that the publisher is not engaged in rendering legal,
accounting, or other professional service. If legal advice or other expert
assistance is required, the services of a competent professional person
should be sought.

Library of Congress Cataloging-in-Publication Data

Whitmire, Richard.
    Why boys fail : saving our sons from an educational system that's leaving them behind / Richard
Whitmire.
        p.   cm.
    Includes index.
    ISBN-13: 978-0-8144-1534-4 (hardcover)
    ISBN-10: 0-8144-1534-2 (hardcover)
    1. Motivation in education. I. Title.

LB1065.W49   2010
370.15′4—dc22   2009031663

Printing number

10 9 8 7 6 5 4 3 2 1

For Robin, Morgan, and Tyler

CONTENTS

FOREWORD

LAST SUMMER I met a twenty-one-year-old high school senior who was struggling to push through his last few credits of high school. He was working with two tutors through a small pilot program targeting students at risk of dropping out. Facing an emotional disability and embarrassed in his summer school classes full of tenth graders, his frequent outbursts meant he was spending more time in the office and on suspension than he was in class.

I met him through a fortunate accident. On one of his trips back to class after a suspension, he happened to overhear the program manager, who was visiting the school that day, from my office, inquiring about a truant student she was trying to pair with a tutor but who was not showing up.

The listening student immediately interjected himself into the conversation and advocated forcefully on his own behalf, convincing the program manager that with a child on the way, and driven by a strong desire to move away from the violence he had seen and been a part of, he was willing to do whatever it would take to earn his diploma, if she would find someone to work with him. As all of our volunteer tutors were assigned already, part of "what it took" involved riding his bike to my office every day where my staff members had volunteered to work with him.

In *Why Boys Fail*, Robert Whitmire has hit not only on the root of this student's challenges and their impact on his life and choices, but on the ways that his challenges weave through the stories of millions of boys in this country. This student's tutors—one in English and one in chemistry—quickly learned that his biggest challenge was literacy.

Many school districts are addressing early literacy deficiencies, but building literacy has to continue throughout the grades, and it must include developmentally appropriate materials for teenagers who are still at an elementary reading level, as our summer school student was. Twice as many boys as girls are classified as special education students. Boys in the D.C. public schools fall behind girls by about nine percentage points in reading and five in math (DC Comprehensive Assessment System/DC CAS). Of our incarcerated youth, 97 percent are boys. Without the reading and writing skills they need to tackle other course areas, either their frustrations come out in the classroom, they begin to shut down, or they drop out.

Our student last summer faced a tenth-grade book while reading at an estimated fifth-grade reading level. He was intelligent and could pick up concepts quickly when they were explained to him. The chemistry textbook was especially daunting, and even with a tutor, the reading was painstaking. In English, he was required to read a novel set in World War II, and he found many connections between the characters' discussions and the streets of Washington, D.C. But even with a strong identification with the characters, he had to read it out loud, slowly, and with intensive one-on-one support to discuss the vocabulary and connections to his experiences.

He discovered that he loved new vocabulary words, and he drank them in as if they were water. After one conversation about narrative voice in fiction, he had to be convinced not to tattoo "omniscient" on his arm! But even with his excitement about his increasing literacy skills, he was no picnic for his principal, teachers, or tutors. Bright and self-aware, he knew he did not have the skills he had trusted us as adults to give him. He was angry.

It was clear that his display of this anger during instruction appeared or intensified when he faced a task he did not suspect he could do. When he feared he would not succeed, he would curse, refuse, or go silently angry. With much of the work requiring a greater level of literacy than he had, this meant more than a few awkward incidents for visitors to the chancellor's office that summer.

But in the end he was true to his word. He put in the hours, and his tutors split the teaching of everything from phonemic awareness to ionic bonds (they may have missed a meeting or two!). He read the novel, wrote the paper, and passed his tests in chemistry and English, literally sweating through his last two courses of high school.

He made it—and I got to shake his hand and congratulate him as he walked across the stage.

But why did it have to be so difficult for him, and for the millions of other young men like him?

There are countless factors other than literacy that can impact boys' achievement, and what is impressive about Whitmire's analysis is that, without oversimplifying this socially, politically, and academically complex issue, he addresses them all while narrowing our focus on the root of literacy that links them all.

Even with a high school diploma, as Whitmire shows is true for millions of boys who graduate without the skills they need, our summer student also has had a difficult time finding and keeping a job, despite the continued coaching he has received. He checks in every month or two, and on his latest visit he picked up a book to continue increasing his reading skills until he will be able to handle the coursework of college.

But like the statistics Whitmire cites throughout *Why Boys Fail*, every day our graduate faces earning a living without the literacy skills he needs—in this economy, a challenge even for those who got what they needed from their school systems. He is now a father, and while I hope he continues to turn away from the options in his neighborhood that compete with us for young men's attention and will, I also know it is a daily struggle and choice.

There is no reason he or the other boys like him should have fallen so far behind. We have access to reams of research and best practices on how to teach children to read and write according to individual needs and learning styles. But we do not definitively know why we are not doing it for boys across the country, and when it comes to children, it is always worth it to find out.

Whitmire illustrates beyond a doubt that the student who studied in my office last summer is far from alone. As adults—whether professionals in education, or simply parents trying to do right by our kids—we spend much of our time and energy battling with the forces that compete for boys' attention, often luring them away from achieving according to their astonishing potential.

It does not have to be this hard. If we do our jobs right from the time boys are young, teaching reading and writing in ways that engage boys, it does not have to be a competition, and parents will not have to wring their hands wondering what went wrong, or feel their hearts break watching their sons fall short of dreams they are perfectly capable of achieving.

Michelle Rhee
Chancellor, District of Columbia Public Schools
Washington, D.C.

ACKNOWLEDGMENTS

HUDDLED IN A chilly mountain inn in Australia's Blue Mountains, I listened to the spooky calls of cockatoos in the surrounding forest and wondered if my research into U.S. boys falling behind in school had gone astray. Why was I here in Australia, a two-hour train ride out of Sydney, rather than visiting more American schools? The journey that brought me to this unusual location started a decade ago when I realized that, contrary to the conventional wisdom among educators and parents, boys—not girls—were the ones struggling in school.

My investigation into the issue started slowly and picked up speed with a reporting fellowship from the University of Maryland that allowed me to travel. I quickly discovered that gender gaps are international and that several countries, including Australia, are ahead of the United States in probing the causes. Eventually, that led me to the Blue Mountains of Australia, home to the Blue Mountains Grammar School in Wentworth Falls, one of scores of schools across Australia where teachers are redesigning schools to buck up the boys who, like the boys in the United States, are lagging well behind the girls. Much of what I learned from this investigation can be found at my website and blog, whyboysfail.com.

Those who read my blog and freelance pieces might guess that the gender gap is my only education interest. Actually, I write about a lot of other issues, including preschools, charter schools, and teacher quality. The boys issue, however, is the only one I blog on and the only issue I've researched deeply enough to justify writing a book. The reason I've poured special attention into the boy troubles is simple: Far too many teachers and parents have it wrong.

Those who doubt that boys are in trouble err by looking at the White House and Wall Street, both dominated by men. Instead, they should be looking at college graduation ceremonies, the pipeline to tomorrow's workforce. There, the gender imbalances favoring women are startling. Just as troubling, those who acknowledge that boys are in trouble often settle on the wrong reasons. Railing against hip-hop music, feminists, or video games won't make a dent in the boy troubles. Settling both those issues—whether and why boys are in trouble—are the book's cornerstones.

Naturally, I received some help and encouragement along the way, starting with my wife, Robin, and my two daughters, Morgan and Tyler. It may seem odd that a father to two daughters would become so interested in the boys issue. But seeing this issue through their eyes—the brothers, nephews, and male classmates who by comparison always seemed to be coming up short—proved to be invaluable. Other thanks go to the University of Maryland for granting me a fellowship to study the boys issue. My editors at the *USA Today* editorial page, Carol Stevens and Brian Gallagher, allowed me to pursue this issue over several years and numerous editorials. They have never regretted that decision and have proved more than willing to stand up to the criticisms from doubters of the gender gaps.

Most impressive were insightful educators I found along my research path. Given that the boy troubles fall on the wrong side of political correctness, only brave and independent educators dare even probe the issue. When I met Kenneth Hilton he was overseeing testing at a school district outside Rochester, New York. Until a school board president asked why girls were winning all the academic awards, Hilton had never thought much about the boys issue. But once a data hound like Hilton burrows in, there's no stopping him. Hilton's research remains unpublished, but he managed to place his finger on the core issue long before anyone I know. He reminds me of a congressional investigator I got to know who probed construction quality at nuclear plants. It's all in the data, he would tell me as he sat at his Capitol Hill desk surrounded by teetering piles of documents. You just have to look for it—few actually make that effort. He was right.

Tom Mortenson continues to turn out the best national and international research on this issue. I once approached him about co-writing a book on the issue and he replied that he wouldn't know what to cite as the solution. That answer gives me pause, even today. Also deserving of thanks are the school leaders who allowed me into their buildings for extended observations: Duncan Smith at Frankford Elementary in Delaware, Jabali Sawicki at Excellence Boys Charter School in New York City, and Susan Schaeffler and Sarah Hayes at the KIPP Key Academy in Washington, D.C.

In Wilmette, Illinois, Glenn "Max" McGee was a first-rate guide to the research done within his school district. And in Australia, Trevor Barman from the Blue Mountains Grammar School was astonishingly generous in turning over the entire school for my examination. Sara Mead, an honest doubter of the boy troubles, sharpened my arguments by challenging them. Sarcasm, I suppose, has no place in a book acknowledgment, but had the U.S. Department of Education done its job and investigated this problem there would be no need for this book. Given that the department continues to fail in that duty—not a single study is even on the horizon—the book goes forward.

My editors at AMACOM have been exacting in their edits, and my agent, Ted Weinstein, gets a head nod for sticking with me through a sometimes bumpy ride.

The reader will notice that collecting this information was a true journey. I made some reporting trips during the University of Maryland fellowship in 2004–2005. I had a chance to visit Australia in 2007. Other reporting was shoehorned in shortly before publication. The interesting thing to note is that little has changed over those years of research. I first linked up with Ken Hilton in 2004 when he was investigating gender gaps in his school district in a suburb of Rochester, New York. When we last spoke in the spring of 2009, he was superintendent of a rural district in the Catskills. Hilton's report from the Catskills: Girls were seriously outpacing boys there as well. This is not a problem that can be turned around quickly. What's troubling is that, at least in the United States, we've barely begun.

Introduction

BEV MCCLENDON CLEARLY remembers the day she discovered the difficulties boys were having in her elementary school. She and the other parents with children at Pearl Creek Elementary in Fairbanks, Alaska, had gathered for the spring awards ceremony. Nestled into a wooded hillside and surrounded by homes that overlook the Alaska Range to the south, Pearl Creek is a school with a dream location and a student body to match. With the University of Alaska as a neighbor, the school draws the children of professors as well as the sons and daughters of Fairbanks's doctors and lawyers. Parents here have ambitious plans for their children, which makes the spring awards day a big event. This day[1] had a beautiful start. The birch trees had greened up the week before and temperatures rose enough to hold the picnic for the sixth graders outside.[2] Following the picnic about 150 parents filed into the school to sit on folding chairs facing a tiny elevated stage. Sitting to the side on bleachers were the sixth graders about to be honored. As the principal called out the awards, often given in clusters, the honored students climbed the stage to receive their awards.

"It was very visual," said McClendon. "You would see one, two, three, four girls climb up to the stage and then walk off. And then another three or four girls would be called up. Here were all these little girls getting the awards." Of the roughly twenty awards given out, it was pretty much a clean sweep of academic awards for the girls that day. Wait, two boys won a "most improved" and a third boy got a good sense of humor/positive attitude award. Ouch. McClendon remembers saying to herself, "Oh, that's horrible."

It's not as if the school didn't see this coming. In the days prior to the awards ceremony, school counselor Annie Caulfield realized she had a problem. Awards that normally went to one boy and girl, such as the

American Legion prize, were instead going to two girls. The prospect of a potentially embarrassing girl sweep caused Caulfield to check on past awards. "Over the last eight years we've seen gradual changes, with more girls winning, and then 'bam.' This year was so blatant, so one-sided. I encouraged the teachers to go back and look again, but they felt this is what it needed to be." What keeps boys off awards stages is a combination of academics and behavior; they don't earn perfect grades and they are more prone to playground tussles. While those boy/girl differences have held for decades, something has happened in recent years to accelerate the problem.

McClendon has few regrets her son didn't get an award that day. He gets plenty of accolades. But what about the other smart boys at Pearl Creek? Other parents of boys, especially those with younger boys in the school, appeared worried that day. "I'm a staunch feminist, but my God look at what they're doing. You can't tell me there were no boys in that school who deserved an award."

To avoid this situation in the future, school officials faced a dilemma: either they start practicing affirmative action for boys or suspend the awards ceremony. They chose the latter. Pushing the problem from public view to avoid another embarrassing clean-sweep ceremony, however, falls short of a long-term solution. This is not a local problem confined to Pearl Creek Elementary. Boys falling behind in school are both a national and international phenomenon involving far more than playground rough-housing. In the United States, the problem is most obvious in high-poverty urban schools, where boys are losing sight of the girls. In Chicago, the girls at Gen. George Patton Elementary School outpaced the boys by fifty-five points on the 2007 state reading tests.[3] Boys are four and a half times as likely as girls to get expelled from preschool and four times as likely to suffer from attention-deficit disorders. In state after state, boys are slipping behind girls in math scores on state exams—which steps on all the conventional wisdom about boys excelling in math—while falling far behind girls in reading. And while the problem is most serious in poor neighborhoods, the awards day snapshot offered up by the upper-income

Pearl Creek Elementary is mirrored in middle- and upper-middle-income schools around the country.

Most worrisome, boys' academic ambitions have skidded. As recently as 1980 more male than female high school seniors planned to graduate from college, federal surveys of high school seniors told us. By 2001, however, girls moved ahead of boys on that question by a startling eleven percentage points (updates to that survey show the gap persists).[4] What happened to boys in those twenty-one years? Answering that question is what this book is about. Those flagging ambitions explain the dramatic gender imbalances unfolding on most college campuses, many of which hover near a 60–40 balance favoring women on graduation day. Why are the gender imbalances worse on graduation day? Because men are both less likely to enroll and more likely to drop out before earning degrees.

The journey to find the answer to the question of why this is happening began more than a decade ago when, like every other education reporter at the time, I bought into the reports that schools were treating girls unfairly, shunting them aside in favor of aggressive boys thrusting their arms into the air to answer teachers' questions. As the father of two girls, I was outraged, and I wrote those stories uncritically. By hindsight, we now know that that research was flawed. I was wrong to write those stories. As my own daughters matured past the elementary school years, I began to witness just how wrong those reports were. My nephews never seemed to fare as well as my nieces. The brothers of our daughters' friends rarely did as well as their sisters. The proof was playing out in the college enrollment and graduation numbers, where women increasingly dominated: Boys, not girls, were the ones struggling in school; men, not women, were falling behind in college graduation numbers. And these are not just poor minority boys falling behind. Plenty of them come from schools such as Pearl Creek Elementary.

* * *

Thanks to a reporting fellowship at the University of Maryland, I began a query into this issue that would persist for many years and include the launching of a website/blog, whyboysfail.com. I quickly discovered that the boy troubles are international and that several countries, including Australia, are far ahead of the United States in probing the roots of the mystery. The journey to answer the question of why boys suddenly lose interest in school eventually led me to Australia, where the government sponsors research that schools use to buck up the boys, who, like the boys in the United States, lag well behind the girls. In just one year, using techniques such as switching to a reading program that relies more on phonics, breaking the curriculum into manageable "chunks" to help the organizationally challenged boys, introducing some single-sex classrooms, and arranging parent-teacher conferences well before exams rather than after the tests to give parents a heads up if their children were in trouble, Blue Mountains Grammar evened out the gender imbalances among its best students.

At Blue Mountains Grammar, these were not trial-and-error experiments. Rather, they were based on results of a federal investigation into the boy problems that were released in 2003. The cause of the boy troubles Australian investigators settled on is relatively uncomplicated and mirrors the cause already identified by Britain, Canada, New Zealand, and other countries that have researched the issue: The world has become more verbal, and boys haven't. Boys lack the literacy skills to compete in the Information Age, a theme that will be explored in greater depth in later chapters. College has become the new high school, and the currencies of any education after high school are verbal skills and the ability to read critically and write clearly. That explains both the recent nature of the problem and its occurrence in so many countries around the world. The lack of literacy skills, especially the ability to write well, also helps explain why fewer men go to college and, once there, are less likely than women to earn degrees.

The boy problems in Australia aren't any worse than the boy problems in the United States. They appear quite similar, as do the boy problems in other Western countries. What makes the United States unique is its relative indifference to the issue. Here, the U.S. Department of Education has yet to launch a single probe into the problem. No doubt, the department is influenced by critics who say the gender gaps are just another manifestation of the long-standing problems of race and poverty. As a separate issue, the "boy troubles" are mostly a myth, they argue. It's true that the gender gaps are starkest in the large urban school districts. In July 2009 the Center for Labor Market Studies at Northeastern University released a study that tracked the students who graduated from Boston Public Schools in 2007. The conclusion: For every 167 women in four-year colleges there were only 100 males. Is poverty the cause? The male and female students came from identical homes and neighborhoods. Is race the issue? That's not what the study uncovered. In fact, black females were five percentage points more likely to pursue any further study after high school—community colleges, four-year colleges, or technical/vocational schools—than white males.

"Public policy concern over these gender gaps has been quite minimal to date," said Andrew Sum, director of the Center. "The issue needs immediate attention given the dramatic consequences these gender gaps have for men's earnings, their marital possibilities, the share of children being raised in single-parent families, and the fiscal outlook for the nation."[5]

And yet parents and schools get no help from the federal education department, leaving local educators on their own as they struggle with faltering boys. Worse, parents and educators are forced to sort through the swarm of what's-wrong-with-boys books, magazine articles, seminars, and TV shows. There's no shortage of solutions offered up by experts. Problem is, my reporting suggests that most of the solutions are inadequate. Parents lose regardless of which "solution" they choose.

Step into any teachers' lounge and you'll hear the usual explanations for the gender gap: Boys mature slower. Girls' brains are hardwired to be better book learners. And then there are toxic-culture explanations: The lure of rap music and Grand Theft Auto traps boys but not girls, they explain. Others point fingers at the larger society, saying that boys' unquestioning embrace of male-macho values stifles the introspection needed to develop verbal skills. One theory that wins a lot of chin nodding both inside and outside teachers' lounges is the anti-academic message of hip-hop culture. Some researchers can even chart the overlap of the rise in hip-hop and the decline in classroom performance of black males.

That's only a down payment on the list of the suggested triggers behind the boy troubles. Check any topic listing of popular magazines or books about the boy troubles and you'll see even more: It's the disappearance of male teachers; it's a need for single-sex classrooms. Many of the explanations come complete with charts, graphs, and dramatic snapshots of the male brain in action: Boys are falling behind as a result of schools failing to embrace "brain-based" learning theories about how boys and girls absorb information in entirely different ways, we are told, a prescription that comes complete with recommended classroom temperatures. Boys, we're advised, prefer cold, dark classrooms. (That actually makes sense, given that it pretty much describes the cold, cluttered home-office study where I'm writing this.) Other explanations require a background in Freud to truly comprehend: Boys are falling behind because mothers cut the apron strings too early, we're told, leaving needy sons bereft of the nurturing love they so badly need, which dooms some to spin out of control.

Most theories about boys falling behind have some truth to them, but until American educators agree on the primary cause of the boy troubles, they risk wasting their time. Let me offer a typical example of how local educators explain the growing gender imbalances. In January 2009, the *Pittsburgh Tribune-Review* ran a story about more women than men going to college in that state:[6]

> In 2007, some 78 percent of Pennsylvania's female high school graduates chose to attend two- and four-year colleges as opposed to the slightly less than 68 percent of boys who did so, according to the state Department of Education.

Until the 1980s, more men than women attended and graduated from college. But by the 1990s, women had caught up, and soon they overtook men.

The article gets interesting when the reporter attempts to answer the "why" question. Two reasons, local education experts say: Girls mature faster and women need college degrees more than men. This is their logic? As the article pointed out, the entire phenomenon of boys falling behind is only about twenty years old. In that brief time frame boys suddenly became less mature? The economic explanation, that women need college more than men, makes more sense and until recent years was true. Women did get a greater salary boost from a degree. The changing economy of today, however, has altered that, and it holds true now only on the anecdotal level. According to the data experts at both the federal Education Department and College Board, men and women today get exactly the same benefits from a college degree.[7]

The point is not to pick on Pennsylvania educators but rather to illustrate the lack of insight in this country about the boy troubles. In Australia, when insightful educators decide to do something about boys lagging behind, they can draw on reams of government research about why it is happening and what can help. They can also apply for a government grant to launch remedies. Now contrast that with what happens in the United States when local teachers or principals decide to do something about the boy troubles. I'll answer that by relating the story of a trip I made to a tiny town in New Mexico, where I learned of a teacher who decided to do something about the boys struggling in his classroom.

THE POJOAQUE STORY

Anyone making the hot, high-speed drive from Santa Fe to Los Alamos passes through the tiny town of Pojoaque, which in Tewa means "water drinking place," an odd name given that Pojoaque is surrounded by dry riverbeds most of the year. Pojoaque (rhymes with Milwaukee) is an all-around unremarkable place. Even the Native American–run casino looks drab and deserted. As a result, drivers probably don't notice the middle school buildings on the right just after leaving the highway to head for the distant mountains that frame Los Alamos. And they would never guess that inside one of those fifth grade classrooms, Paul Ortiz is running an education experiment that for New Mexico is pretty exciting stuff: all-boy classes in math and reading.

Ortiz's single-sex experiment was born of a quirk. One night as he was grading papers he realized he needed some background noise to concentrate and tuned in PBS. "I figured it would be some British movie, which for me is not very interesting." Instead, Ortiz started listening to a documentary by *Raising Cain*[8] author Michael Thompson, who was talking about the problems boys were having in school. "Needless to say I was hooked."

Ortiz knew all about boys having trouble in school. The year before, he had had twelve boys in his class, half of them labeled as special education. "When I looked at these boys they didn't seem like special education students." But when Ortiz checked with the front office he learned that was roughly average for the boys in the intermediate school—and about five times the rate for girls.

Ortiz was convinced the boys in his school were more reluctant learners than true special education students, and the PBS documentary gave him the idea he could do something for the boys of Pojoaque. "I came into the school and spoke to some people about it and the librarian told me that *Newsweek* had just published something about that." In the *Newsweek*[9] cover story about the problems boys were having, Ortiz read about a Colorado school experimenting with single-sex education. Michael Thompson had cited single-sex classes as beneficial to boys in his PBS special. "I looked into it further and found it was legal to offer single-sex education in public schools. I took two months to do as much research as possible and then wrote up a proposal and gave it to my principal, who was interested."

Eventually, Ortiz was able to launch his single-sex experiment. But what's striking about this story is that Ortiz had to figure out everything himself. It was up to Ortiz to point out that boys were having unique problems in schools and then craft a solution—even though boys everywhere in New Mexico are falling behind, not just in Pojoaque. On national tests, between 10 and 18 percent more boys than girls in New Mexico K–12 schools score "below basic" in reading and writing. Sixty percent of the girls graduate from high school, compared to 53.5 percent of the boys. Sixty-six percent of the students in special education are boys. Sixty percent of the students held back each year are boys.[10] As has happened in the rest of the country, the K–12 problems in New Mexico are spilling over into college. Over just the past ten years the percentage of males receiving bachelor's degrees at public universities in that state fell from 45 percent to 41 percent.

Given the magnitude of the problem, it's troubling that Ortiz was forced to rely on tidbits gleaned from a TV show and a *Newsweek* cover story. Especially worrisome is that his school district, the state education department, and the U.S. Department of Education had no advice to offer him in setting up an intervention for the boys. All this leaves Ortiz as isolated as Pojoaque itself. "Yeah, I'm pretty much on my own," concedes the soft-spoken Ortiz. "It's kind of scary at times." What he came up with—single-sex classrooms, boy-friendly reading materials, and a freedom to move around a bit—seemed to be working during my visit in 2007; it was too soon for anyone to know, including Ortiz. In the spring of 2009, when I checked on Ortiz's efforts, I heard good news, with the all-boys classes (and all-girls classes) outpacing the school average.

Ortiz appears to have chosen an educational path that is paying off. But Ortiz and other educators determined to level the gender gaps shouldn't have to conduct trial-and-error experiments on their own. We owe them an Australian-style federal investigation into the cause of the problem. The Aussies are a long way from solving the gender gaps. As I learned from the visit there, schools such as Blue Mountains Grammar are the exception. Most aren't taking the government up on its offer to work on the problem. But at least the Australians, starting six years ago, got schools willing to tackle the problem on an intelligent path. In this country, we remain years away from even reaching the starting line to begin working on the problem.

* * *

The absence of federal attempts to deal with boys' lagging academic ambitions creates an opening for a journalist to step in and evaluate what is being offered up to parents and educators about the boy troubles. I will sort through the theories, weigh the evidence, and offer an opinion. Always, I will try to stick with what reporters do best, which is investigate. And I will abide by my Missouri roots: Show me. When I find schools where boys and girls both succeed at academics, I will draw lessons about what happens in those schools that is not happening in the many schools where boys lag far behind. In the end, readers can decide for themselves what their neighborhood schools are doing, or not doing, on behalf of their sons. To get started, let's look at what we know about boys falling behind in school.

C H A P T E R

Discovering the Problem

A QUICK WALK down Main Street in Farmington, Maine, reveals a New England college town cute enough to qualify for central casting. There's the Liquid Sunshine store, which sells long, flowing skirts. Close by is Calico Patch, peddling candles and objets d'arts freshmen women buy to adorn their dorm rooms at the University of Maine, Farmington, located only a couple of blocks away. Next comes Outskirts, offering vintage clothing for women. Finally, there is Butterfly Boutique, a purveyor of pricey clothing that senior co-eds purchase for their first real-world job interview.[1]

Within a couple of blocks, you realize what feels odd about the walk through town. Stores in downtown Farmington target only female college students. Not much for the guys to be found anywhere. But what at first appears to be an oversight turns out to be nothing more than business common sense: Two-thirds of the students studying at the Farmington campus are women. Women here dominate both the shopping scene downtown and the leadership positions on campus. They serve as presidents of most of the campus clubs and occupy seven of the eight spots on the student program board that arranges student activities. The male students here don't seem to mind. They think they've achieved dating heaven. "That's one reason I came here," admitted one freshman as he tilted far back in his dorm chair. Surrounded by cardboard boxes stuffed with finger food snacks and a giant video screen used mostly for video games, he and his four male friends exchange satisfied smiles. Life is *sweet*, they told me.

The growing majorities of women on college campuses may delight freshman guys, but they trigger worries among others nervously watching the trend. While most colleges aren't as female-concentrated as Farmington, they're moving in that direction, with average graduating classes at four-year colleges approaching 60 percent women. The college graduation rate favoring women shows no sign of abating, with women overtaking men at every level, from associate to Ph.D. The fact that women who enter college are far more likely than their male classmates to earn a degree only worsens the problem. Those growing imbalances leave college officials wrestling with multiple problems: overcrowded women's bathrooms in co-ed dorms, classrooms where only female voices are heard in discussions, and lost tuition from boys who should be attending college.

Most alarmed about the slipping ratios of men on college campuses are marketplace economists, who point out that in the Information Age college has become the new high school. Nearly everyone needs some kind of post–high school training, even those aiming for blue-collar jobs that don't require four-year degrees. "The days are over when you could walk into a paper mill with a high school diploma and run one of the machines," said Patrick Schillinger of the Wisconsin Paper Council.[2] Want to be a bank teller or work behind an airport rental car counter? A generation ago, high school graduates filled those jobs. No longer. At a minimum, tellers need an associate's degree. And those seemingly noncomplex jobs of checking off the little boxes required for renting a car are going to four-year degree holders. Companies today recognize that these jobs require a level of people skills, writing ability, and basic math competence found only among those with college training. That economic shift is why the Obama Administration set a new goal in the summer of 2009 of having all students go to college for at least one year.

In April 2009, in the middle of a brutal recession, California employment experts concluded the state faced a shortage of one million college graduates needed for the workforce in 2025. By that year, a minimum of 41 percent of all jobs will require college degrees while only 35 percent of the state's working-age adults will hold four-year degrees.[3] The U.S. Department of Labor estimated that 80 percent of the fastest growing jobs of the twenty-first century will require postsecondary education or training. And yet, of every one hundred ninth graders, only sixty-eight will graduate from high school on time, only forty will directly enter college, and only twenty-seven will still be enrolled their sophomore year. Finally, among those one hundred, only eighteen will graduate within six years.[4] And if those figures were sorted by gender, boys would dominate each fallout point. Men need these degrees as much as women, and yet somehow only women are responding logically to the education demands of this new economy. That leaves tens of thousands of otherwise talented boys stalled at the starting gates, unable to win entry-level jobs in the new economy. If anything, the urgency for men to acquire more post–high school training has accelerated. More than 80 percent of those laid off during the global recession that began in 2008 were men. By the spring of 2009, as the recession deepened and the layoffs continued, women became the majority of the workforce.

How could a societal change as significant as boys falling so far behind girls in academic ambitions come about so quietly and quickly? Until that question gets answered, any school interventions drawn up to help boys will be based on little more than guesswork.

Given the lack of federal interest in the boy problems, school leaders are left on their own to discover the problem. Some important clues emerge from their discoveries. In 2001 Kenneth Dragseth, the superintendent of schools in Edina, Minnesota, a wealthy and mostly white suburb of Minneapolis, noticed something odd playing out in the high school academic awards ceremonies he attended. Nearly all the awards, as well as the college scholarships, went to girls. It struck Dragseth as a new phenomenon. Just a few years earlier the boys were pulling down an equal share of the awards. Dragseth ordered an investigation and the next year received a report with these conclusions: Girls made up 65 percent of the honor rolls and won 67 percent of the top-of-the-class rankings. Boys, by contrast, accounted for nine out of every ten school suspensions and more than seven in ten of these students were taking medication for attention-deficit hyperactivity disorder. The Edina investigation failed to pinpoint a cause, but it did offer a clue: 84 percent of the girls said they liked school, compared to 64 percent of the boys. And far more girls than boys reported doing daily homework. In short, Dragseth's survey discovered that schooling agrees more with girls. Edina is not the only wealthy white community to discover that, contrary to conventional wisdom, the boy problems are not limited to African-American boys living in poverty and attending failing schools.[5] Here's a story about another upper-class public school discovering what Dragseth found in his schools.

THE WILMETTE DISCOVERY

Glenn "Max" McGee may be a professional educator, but for him, discovering the gender gaps among middle school–age boys was a personal matter. When McGee was serving as state superintendent of schools of Illinois he saw the problem develop with his own two sons. "Their interest in reading fell off around the fifth and sixth grades. The same was happening with their interest in writing and keeping a journal. They were in a good school system and they liked school, but their desire and joy for reading and writing were evaporating. Our oldest had more of an 'attitude' and our youngest was becoming apathetic, and here I was, state superintendent of schools. I remember thinking: 'This can't be my family.' "

McGee's family education problems coincided with a report from the American Association of University Women (AAUW)[6] charging that school districts were neglecting girls, especially in math and science. McGee recalls embracing the report and doing everything he could do to correct what, at the time, appeared to be a major issue. "I was active in trying to close gender gaps in math and science for girls. I spoke on behalf of the AAUW. But all the time I realized we were having these issues with reading and writing with boys."

In 2002 McGee took over as superintendent of the K–8 Wilmette schools along Chicago's high-income North Shore, right on the doorstep of Northwestern University. These schools feed into the famed New Trier

High School, which rests high on any top ten list of America's best public high schools. McGee sat down to map out a way to accomplish what he describes as making the great schools there even greater. Based on his own family experience, McGee had a hunch: Let's look at boosting boys' performance. To the Wilmette educators, this was a radical approach. Who thought the boys had any problems?

To carry out the boys investigation McGee needed the help of the Community Review Committee (CRC), a panel of administrators, teachers, and parents that takes on issues day-to-day educators are too busy to tackle. In Wilmette, possibly one of the wealthiest and most education-focused school districts in the United States, these inquiries are taken *very* seriously. Within the committee there was considerable skepticism about looking at boys as a problem area. In this case, committee members were given a choice: Join the boys "gender study" task force or work on a second investigation into the far less controversial topic of how student progress gets reported to parents. Nearly all the CRC members chose the latter. The boy/girl panel was left with four parents and less than a handful of administrators and teachers. But what a handful it turned out to be. Among the four parents were three past presidents of the CRC.

Cochairing the task force was a father of two boys, an MIT-trained numbers guy with a broad business background currently working in private equity advising. Also on the panel was Diane Fisher, a mother of two boys who has a Ph.D. in clinical psychology. "There was an enormous amount of resistance to us looking at this," she recalls. "The others saw it as a hot-button issue and they didn't want to use the word 'gender.' They wanted to look at learning differences in general and not make it into a gender issue. I think it was really political discomfort for them. And a number of these parents didn't really believe these gender differences exist. We were like a little band of outlaws."

Overseeing the research was McGee himself, who of course brought along his personal experience as the father of two boys who had watched both boys lose their interest in reading after about fifth grade. And so, after a rocky beginning, the committee got under way. Part of the task force's research included a survey of 270 teachers asking if the teachers thought there was any reason to suspect gender imbalances in the district. Are either boys or girls earning better grades? The response: 85 percent said they were not aware of any gender gaps. Only three teachers speculated that girls might be doing better than boys.

In June 2006 the task force released its 107-page report. In stark contrast to what the teachers thought was happening, the task force found "surprising" gender gaps. In grades five through eight, girls had higher grades than boys in every core subject, including math. "It appears that girls have figured out how to get good grades, and as they experience success, they continue to be rewarded for behaviors that are valued," said the task force. Even more surprising was the finding that the performance gap between boys and girls widened in each of the three years they studied. Plus, most of the problem students were boys. Boys made up the "overwhelming majority" of the discipline referrals and suspensions, the report concluded, along with 71 percent of the special education students.

As it turned out, McGee's hunch about the boys being in trouble was well founded. "What surprised us the most," said the father who cochaired the panel, "is that in every one of the subjects we looked we found gender gaps in grades, without exception, even in subjects where boys usually test better. Some of the biggest differences we found were in advanced math in junior high, where girls were doing better." Just as surprising were the trend lines. In junior high school, where they could gather four years of data, the grade-point advantage enjoyed by girls had grown in each of the four years. "The grade-point gap grew in all eleven subjects, and it grew significantly in nine of the eleven."

Among the report findings:

- Girls are 30 to 35 percent more likely to earn an A.

- In grades five through eight, girls' grades were higher than boys across reading, writing, science, and math. In every level of junior high math, girls have outperformed boys, across four years of data and four levels of math.

- On the Iowa Test of Basic Skills, girls outperform boys across seven language arts scores.

- Seventy-one percent of the district's special education population is male.

- Boys make up the "overwhelming majority" of discipline referrals.

Keep in mind, the survey of teachers taken before the research indicated they overwhelmingly believed there were no gender gaps. These were the same teachers who were handing out better grades to girls in each of the subjects in each grade. "It was a real surprise," says McGee. "We have terrific students, outstanding parents, and plenty of resources. And yet there are these differences."

IS WILMETTE ALONE?

Parents there appeared shocked by the report. Nobody thought this could happen in Wilmette. "We have very high-achieving parents," said Fisher, "who serve as strong role models. They provided enriched experiences for these boys since the day they were born. Travel, private tutors, coaches. If you think about it, any check that could have been written to put these boys on the same playing field with the girls was written. All that was done, and yet it still does not change the neurological development reality. If you see this in an affluent district such as Wilmette, how is it for boys who haven't had all these advantages?"

In Wilmette, nearly everyone eventually goes to college, even the slacker boys, which raises the question of whether boys lagging behind in

K–12 even matters. The uneven academic track does matter, said the businessman/dad who cochaired the panel. The process of what goes on day to day in classrooms is as important as the product, which is college attendance, he explains. "I see my boys, even in middle school, making choices. Their educational experiences inform those choices. We are nothing more than a cumulative set of those choices. So how educators interact with kids and encourage the development of those choices has profound implications for the ultimate paths they pick." And what he sees is a lot of boys making choices that will limit their future. By choosing to eschew reading and devalue writing, they are removing themselves from the competition for business jobs that involve communicating, writing, client relations, and bringing institutions together to achieve a common interest. In short, they are removing themselves from jobs such as he has held. Women can take those same jobs, but that removes a sizable chunk of society from even joining the competition. "The problem is that as a society we are saying we are going down a path where the education processes have the effect of statistically excluding a portion of the population."

The task force members wondered if other well-off districts were discovering similar gender gaps, but they soon discovered other educators simply weren't looking for it. Most school districts fall into that category. They don't know the extent to which their boys are falling behind because they've never bothered to look. According to the new annual state exams launched to meet the requirements of the federal No Child Left Behind Act, the boys are indeed falling behind, especially in literacy skills. But if school districts never look, there's no chance they'll find the problem.

THE CLUE EVERYONE MISSED: THE NINTH GRADE "BULGES"

Many high school principals are seeing a phenomenon something akin to a fog-induced interstate pileup, in which boys pile up in ninth grade, with many of them never making it as far as tenth grade. This "bulge," as educators call it, appears to have grown out of the school reform movement that dates back to the 1989 governors' summit in Charlottesville, Virginia. As a result of the college push agreed upon at the summit, nearly every ninth grader now gets a verbally drenched curriculum that is supposed to better prepare them for post–high school study.

The governors' goals were perfectly sensible; these are the new realities of the global economy. But a problem soon emerged. By ramping up the literacy demands but failing to give boys the tools they need to meet those demands, the modest, birth-granted verbal advantages enjoyed by girls have widened considerably. Ninth grade is when that problem becomes visible. As school districts raised standards, principals came under pressure to make their schools look better on the state tests. So if a ninth grader is stumbling through math and English, wouldn't it be better to have that student repeat ninth grade? The alternative, having that student fail the state's tenth grade tests and give the school a black eye, is something most principals would prefer to avoid.

Thus was born the bulge, where ninth grade classes run larger than either eighth or tenth grade classes. The bulge numbers are staggering. In 2006 the Atlanta-based Southern Regional Education Board (SREB) released data[7] measuring the bulge using a simple tool: Compare the size of the eighth grade against the size of the ninth grade. In Florida, the ninth grade was 19 percent larger; in Maryland 17 percent; in Texas 17 percent; in Georgia 16 percent. Not surprisingly, those bulges contain twice as many boys as girls. "This bulge is going to be largely driven by retention in grade and boys are twice as likely to fail as girls," said Joan Lord, director of educational policies for the SREB. "The students are not prepared for high school; they're failing classes and therefore being retained." Due to retentions in previous grades, the boys arrive in ninth grade close to the age when they can legally drop out of school, an age that varies by state from sixteen to nineteen. "At that point many of them are losing motivation, the will to finish. They see that if they wait it out they can quit so they just sort of give up in ninth grade and wait it out," said Lord.

What Lord describes explains the high dropout rates educators only recently discovered in ninth grade. Previously, they believed the dropout problem was far worse in the upper grades. Florida educators, for example, discovered that half their dropouts leave school before their sophomore year.[8] The obvious reason boys flounder in ninth grade is a lack of academic preparation for the college-prep classes required in high school, a problem that dates back to the early grades. Many of the boys being retained are seen as discipline problems when in fact their problems are academic. Explained one principal from Jackson, Mississippi, "Sometimes, when guys don't understand a concept they become discipline problems. It's a lot easier to be disciplined for talking back to the teacher than to be embarrassed in front of the class because you can't read."

Another explanation for the ninth grade bulge also dates back to the education reforms launched from that 1989 governors' conference in Charlottesville: high-stakes testing. When schools get judged on how many students pass state tests, they find ways of sidetracking kids likely to make their school look bad. "You find this bulge is highest in states with high-stakes assessments, usually in tenth grade," said Gene Bottoms, who runs the respected High Schools That Work program with SREB. "You don't have to be a rocket scientist to figure out which kids are going to score lower on those tests. You warehouse them in grade nine." Most schools make an honest attempt to do something with their faltering ninth graders, including the boys. But those interventions rarely prove to be clear winners. One of the few surveys aimed solely at ninth graders was conducted by Gene Bottoms's program. The 2006 survey included 11,500 students in 129 schools in 26 states.

The results:

- 55 percent of the girls reported earning grades of A or B, compared to 41 percent of the boys.

- 49 percent of the girls reported often working hard to meet standards on assignments, compared to 35 percent of the boys.

- 68 percent of the girls reported trying to do their best work in school, compared to half the boys.

- 29 percent of the girls reported often revising essays or other work to improve quality, compared to 16 percent of the boys.

- 68 percent of the girls reported knowing when projects are due, compared to 55 percent of the boys.

- 48 percent of the girls reported trying harder after receiving extra help, compared to 34 percent of the boys.

Those numbers mirror a study released in 2005 done by the Consortium on Chicago School Research that determined which students are "on track" to graduate. That indicator, which roughly mirrors the bulge population, found wide gender gaps. Among African-American students, for example, 60 percent of the girls were on track but only 44 percent of the boys. Among white students, 80 percent of the girls were on track compared to 67 percent of the boys. Among Latinos, 67 percent of the girls were on track, compared to 52 percent of the boys.

In Detroit in 2007, educators desperate to stem the number of ninth grade dropouts began requiring eighth graders to take a college-level "life skills" class. The online course, offered in partnership with a community college, covers note taking, study skills, and career planning. Students can earn one college credit. "We know we're losing students at the ninth grade," said Detroit superintendent William Coleman III. "We want them to come into high school excited about learning."[9]

Whatever is going on with boys in ninth grade, it stretches from inner-city Chicago to the affluent suburban schools, and it's felt in college. When college admissions directors huddle together to commiserate about not finding enough men to recruit to their campuses, they point to a single culprit: ninth grade. Until ninth grade, most boys get passed along from grade to grade regardless of whether they have the literacy skills and organizational habits to cut it in high school. And then comes ninth grade, where boys hit the harsh reality of a college-track curriculum for which they are ill-prepared. The C's and D's the boys earn that year haunt them through high school. Even if they recover by eleventh grade, their grades, compared to the girls' grades, won't measure up. Unless college admissions directors have the authority to practice "gender weighting" (common in private colleges)—admitting boys with lower high school grade-point averages—young men will pay a price.

The ninth grade bulges should have been a big clue for educators that boys were in trouble, but that's not how they were read. Educators are trained to look for clues along the dividing lines of race and income. That's what the law tells them to do, so that's what they do. As a result, the big, fat, glaring gender warning signs of the ninth grade bulges were passed off as the all-too-familiar problem of race and income. And everyone knows those problems are nearly intractable, educators tell us, so they throw up their hands in futility.

THE ACTUAL CAUSES OF THE PROBLEM EMERGE

The warning signs behind the ninth grade bulges were missed by both local and national educators. To date, the U.S. Department of Education has yet to fund a single study looking into boys falling behind. That leaves the mystery for others to solve. One clue to solving the mystery emerges from federal test data dubbed the "nation's report card" but technically called NAEP, for National Assessment of Educational Progress. In 2006, University of Alaska professor Judith Kleinfeld was trying out various combinations of NAEP data when she came across this: At the end of high school, nearly one in four white sons of college-educated parents scored "below basic" on the reading section of the NAEP, compared to 7 percent of their female counterparts. That finding merits a quick pause for contemplation. This means one in every four white high school senior boys, boys with at least one college-educated parent, can't read the local newspaper with "understanding," the official description of what "below basic" means. Not only are these boys incapable of succeeding in college, they risk falling short in technical classes that require understanding complex manuals, a must in many blue-collar jobs. Now the pieces begin to fit together. Over the past several years many states, including Vermont, Kentucky, Washington, Maine, and Maryland, have reported sharp reading differences by gender. In 2005 the *Everett Herald* gained access to the Washington state test data and discovered that 40 percent more boys than girls flunked the state reading exam. In Massachusetts, independent investigators discovered that 41 percent of the state's girls scored proficient on the state reading test, compared to 29 percent of the boys.

All this points to the same problem uncovered in Australia: Boys aren't keeping up with new literacy demands. In this country, the reading pressure on boys picked up when schools responded to the 1989 governors' summit, where it was decided that every student needed to be steered into a college-track curriculum that demands high-level verbal skills.

Most teachers and parents are barely aware of the problem or its source, in part because the nation's cadre of schoolteachers, increasingly female, maintains a traditional "boys will be boys" attitude. Don't worry, they tell parents, eventually your sons will do better in school. Only they don't. Worse yet, those schools that undertake rescue missions to save struggling boys base those missions on misguided notions of what's behind their struggles. Hence, nothing much changes. Therefore, in Chapter 5 I sift through those "notions," an exercise I'll call the blame game. First, however, let's examine the biggest contributor to the gender gaps.

The Reason for the Boy Troubles: Faltering Literacy Skills

IF FORCED to conjure up a single sentence summarizing what I learned researching this book, it would be this: The world has gotten more verbal; boys haven't. To prepare students for a more sophisticated economy, educators wisely pushed a tougher curriculum down through the grades. Preschoolers today are confronted with challenges first graders faced twenty years ago. On the surface, that makes sense, but educators overlooked the fact that young boys aren't wired for early verbal challenges. Using the right reading techniques there's no reason boys can't catch up with girls by between fourth and sixth grades, say reading experts such as William Brozo. That, however, is not happening because teachers never adjusted their techniques to accommodate the boys. In a typical school environment, any child who is five months behind at the end of first grade has only a one-in-five chance of ever catching up to grade level, calculates Joseph Torgesen, director emeritus of the Florida Center for Reading Research at Florida State University. Poor reading skills snowball through the grades. By fifth grade, a child at the bottom of the class reads only about 60,000 words a year in and out of school, compared to a child in the middle of the class who reads about 800,000 words a year.[1]

The fault for boys falling behind can't be laid entirely upon teachers. The "experts" at the district and state level who oversaw this pushdown of the curriculum never realized that ratcheting up standards would backfire on boys. As a result, teachers never got trained to help boys survive these changes. That oversight is proving disastrous to boys who not only don't catch up by the end of elementary school but fall farther behind in middle school. Those broadening gender gaps persist through high school, which explains why more women than men enroll in college and, once there, are more likely to graduate. "Literacy is the currency of college work," argues Thomas Newkirk, an English professor at the University of New Hampshire and author of *Misreading Masculinity*.[2] "Your grading in college is basically based on how well you can write." Somehow, that message has not gotten out. "A lot of boys live by the end run. They think they can screw around in school but if they're aggressive and social the world will take care of them. And for many years the world did take care of them, but that world is gone. There are a lot of boys out there living in a world with expectations that are unrealistic."

COLLEGE HAS BECOME THE NEW HIGH SCHOOL

That's the big picture. Now let's get more specific about how boys are getting hurt by their lagging literacy skills: College has become the new high school. Let me explain with examples. Cops who once needed only a high school degree now need at least an associate's degree, not just to get hired but to acquire the report-writing skills that keep them out of legal trouble. Building contractors need those same writing skills for the same reason. The guy who runs a computerized machine at a paper mill or fixes your Prius has to comprehend manuals that would stump many high-achieving high school seniors with lofty SAT scores aiming for a Dartmouth admittance letter.

In this economy, far more of the decent-paying jobs require some training or degree completion beyond high school. Consider this example from my travels: One snowy February afternoon in 2007 I flew into St. Louis and ended up at the Enterprise rental lot. I was met by a young woman identified only by the first name on her name tag, Lyndsay. She bristled with friendliness, asking me about my visit to St. Louis and my hometown roots. So I asked Lyndsay about her life—a recent graduate of a local university with a degree in marketing. Lyndsay performed well but in all honesty, her job required no advanced skills. She noted the mileage, checked the car for damages, and offered a few simple directions for getting out of the lot. The entire transaction took only a minute or two, requiring no calculus, no deconstruction of Hemingway, no advanced economics. In short, nothing Lyndsay did that morning as a "management trainee" required a college degree.

Curious, I checked with Enterprise's top recruiter and discovered that nearly all the management trainees Enterprise hires have college degrees. Why? "A degree for us says several things," said an Enterprise executive. "It's a commitment to completing a job, an ability to learn and multitask. We're looking for leadership and communication skills." Makes perfect sense. What Lyndsay did that day didn't draw on much of her marketing coursework, but it drew heavily on basic people skills, which is the minimum one would expect from a college graduate. What makes sense for Enterprise makes sense to hundreds of other companies as well. College is the new high school. It's the minimum threshold for finding employees who satisfy customers. That message, however, does not seem to be getting through to the thousands of guys failing to acquire college credentials. Sure, a guy graduating from high school has the skills to check cars for damage and fill out basic paperwork. He may even know more about the inner workings of a car than Lyndsay. But he'll rarely get a chance at Enterprise to display his talents. Companies such as Enterprise have no reason to hire anyone with less than a bachelor's degree. No wonder Enterprise, which as a car company has traditionally been staffed by men, has been hiring more women in recent years.

I'd like to claim I discovered this on my own by process of elimination, but in truth countries such as England and Australia that are years ahead of the United States in examining the boy problems have come to the same conclusion. And yet boys don't seem to be getting the message. Perhaps U.S. high schools need to make required reading of Thomas Friedman's best seller *The World Is Flat*.[3] Friedman expertly lays out the international chess game played by major employers as they move technical chores and investments between countries. As harsh as it may sound, the spoils in this new game go to the best-educated workforce.

The problem, of course, is that boys fall behind well before they're capable of tackling Friedman's world. Frankly, after spending a year researching this, the number of pinch points where boys falter, especially regarding reading skills, would spill off a single-spaced typed page—starting with the possibility of getting expelled from preschool. If a boy somehow survives fifth grade but still lacks strong reading abilities, he's in serious trouble because middle school teachers turn to "literature." Then comes ninth grade, the crunch year, where school officials discover he has fallen too far behind to risk taking the tenth grade state assessment (failing students are an understandable embarrassment to the school rankings), which earns him another go-round at ninth grade. Many boys who make it to their senior year of high school end up with grade-point averages well below those of the girls. Too few boys end up going to college and too few of those who do manage to graduate. College may have become the new high school, but a lot of boys discover that fact too late.

EROSION OF VERBAL SKILLS IS THE KEY

A quick glance at national reading tests illustrates the literacy gap. Over the last twenty years the reading skills of seventeen-year-old boys have been in a steady decline. Each year since 1988 the gap between boys' and girls' reading skills has widened a bit more.[4] It all starts in the earliest grades with schools responding to the demands of the new global marketplace by pushing verbal skills earlier and earlier. "What forty years ago was considered the 'reading readiness' component for first grade is now the Head Start exit criteria for four-year-olds (knowing letter names, how to write the letters, letter sounds, and a few words)," said reading expert Richard Allington, a former president of the International Reading Association. That intensity carries into kindergartens, where many teachers require students to keep journals. Here's the problem for the boys: Those same schools ratcheting up their verbal skills requirements never demanded that teachers adjust their teaching practices to make sure boys kept up with the new pace.

Little boys' brains have never been ideally suited to pick up verbal skills so early in life. But in years past it never mattered. That time is disappearing. Now, boys who don't pick up literacy skills early risk falling behind permanently, or worse. A study by Stanford University researchers found a connection between lagging reading skills and discipline problems that could explain why many educators report rising discipline problems among boys. Many slow readers, said the researchers, eventually come to be seen by their teachers as aggressive. "Relatively low literacy achievement in first grade predicted relatively high aggressive behavior in third grade," concluded the researchers. "It's possible that kids who are poor readers get more and more frustrated over time."[5]

The early focus on reading and writing is just the beginning. The area where boys once excelled, crunching math calculations, has faded from view in most schools, replaced with word problems. Many state math assessments contain nothing but word problems, as do the SAT and ACT college admissions tests. What has gone unnoticed is that many boys can't wade through the puzzling words and long sentences to get to the actual math calculation. When a University of Maryland math professor examined the Maryland algebra exam, he found the text setting up the problem more challenging than the actual problem. Students could know the math but flunk the exam—yet another player in boys falling behind.

HOW BAD IS IT OUT THERE?

It's not good, but in many states parents and teachers are barely aware of the problem because they're not looking for any problems. Take Rhode Island as an example. In 2007 the *Providence Journal* splashed a 1,200-

word article across its front page with the headline "State Worries Too Many Students Have Reading Problems."[6] Indeed, that's the case. As the newspaper graphic showed, children in Providence schools fared the worst, with 54 percent reading below grade level. "We are in a time of raising standards," said Todd Flaherty, deputy commissioner, "and it's the right goal, but we have kids who have no shot at those standards because they can't read."

Good point. But who are those kids in Providence and elsewhere in the state who can't read well enough to keep up with the new standards? The state report pinpointed poor children and English learners. What the article didn't explore, because the state investigators never collected the data, is whether boys make up the bulk of those poor readers. Answering that question takes a bit of detective work on the Rhode Island Department of Education's website, but the answer is there. In the eleventh grade, for example, nearly twice as many boys as girls fall into the lowest reading categories.[7] One can only imagine how that ratio grows in the urban districts such as Providence.

Even a state such as neighboring Massachusetts, which deserves credit as a pioneer for carrying out some of the most successful education reforms in the nation, is just now awakening to the fact that its male students are not reading well enough to keep up. The Rennie Center for Education Research & Policy released a report showing Massachusetts boys well behind the girls.[8] On the highly regarded MCAS test (Massachusetts Comprehensive Assessment System), 41 percent of fourth grade girls scored proficient, compared to 29 percent of the boys, according to the study of the state's ten largest urban school districts. The gender gap didn't improve in the seventh grade, where the percentage of boys failing the exam was nearly double the percentage of girls failing. In the tenth grade, 46 percent of the girls in these districts scored proficient, compared to 36 percent of the boys.

When reporters from the *Everett Herald* won access to Washington's achievement test results for more than 76,000 tenth graders, they discovered that at many schools as many as 40 percent more boys than girls failed the reading section of the test. Said Governor Christine Gregoire, "We really haven't had the focus between males and females, and I think we ought to pay as much attention to that as we do all the other factors."[9] Eventually, that test will determine which students graduate from high school. Had that test been in effect that year, 1,400 more girls than boys would have graduated.[10] (Interestingly, the newspaper investigators also discovered exactly what the Rennie Center researchers found in Massachusetts: Girls had caught up or surpassed the boys in math skills.)

Massachusetts and Washington are not alone. Similar findings have emerged from many states, including Maine, Maryland, Kentucky, and Vermont. The gender gaps in verbal skills appear to be connected to a broader loss in verbal skills. National tests such as the National Assessment of Educational Progress show both girls and boys sliding in verbal skills, with boys slipping faster. Too many high school students are graduating without the reading skills they will need in either college or the workforce, warned Richard Ferguson, chief executive officer of the ACT, which administers the ACT college admissions test.[11]

The combination of low teacher expectations and vague state curriculum guides that don't define reading expectations has left thousands of students unable to read complex texts, which is the threshold for those who can cut it in college. "The impact of low expectations is devastating to students," said Ferguson. "We have a moral imperative to give all students the opportunity to develop critical reading skills in high school." Similar warnings have come from the National Governors Association and National Association of State Boards of Education. Just three in ten eighth graders are proficient readers, and 40 percent of high school graduates lack the literacy skills demanded by employers, warned the governors.[12] About half the incoming ninth graders in high-poverty urban schools read three years or more below grade levels, warned the school boards group.[13]

School districts taking a hard look at the problem of slipping reading scores usually discover that most of the problem lies with boys. New Jersey eighth grade boys test twenty-three percentage points below the girls.[14] In a time of education reform, where most students get steered into a verbal-heavy college preparation curriculum, that means the reading problem worsens in later grades and spills into all classes. "If you go to your local high school, the basic-track classes are dominated by boys, and the AP courses are dominated by girls," said Michael Smith, coauthor of *Reading Don't Fix No Chevys.*[15]

The boy problem shows up in national data as well, and not just among poor and minority boys (the contention of those who try to diminish the boy problems). "Take a look at the reading and writing achievement of boys whom we would most expect to do well, the sons of college-educated parents—your sons and grandsons and the young men available for our daughters to marry," said Judith Kleinfeld, a psychology professor at the University of Alaska Fairbanks and director of Boys Project, a group that advocates interventions for boys.[16] Here's the startling data snapshot Kleinfeld mined from federal tests about the literacy of high school seniors, the young men who have hung in there and not dropped out. I referred to this earlier in the book, but the finding is so key it needs repeating: At the end of high school, 23 percent of the white sons of college-educated parents—almost a quarter—scored "below basic" in reading achievement, compared to only 7 percent of their female counterparts. "That means that almost one in four boys who have college-educated parents cannot read a newspaper with understanding. What kinds of jobs can they get in the Information Age, where not only professionals but also mechanics must be able to read complicated directions?"

The National Assessment of Educational Progress (NAEP) tests are not the only indicator of broad shortcomings in literacy. The National Assessment of Adult Literacy reveals an astonishing gap—only 31 percent of college graduates rate as "proficient" readers. Similar declines were found among Americans with graduate degrees. "[The survey] wasn't trying to measure how well Americans can read *Great Expectations* or *Native Son*," said Sandra Stotsky, a former Massachusetts Department of Education official who evaluated the data from the perspective of men versus women. "If it had, the decline might have been even greater. To the contrary, the assessment sought to find out how well adults read basic instructions and can do such tasks as comparing viewpoints in two editorials and reading prescription labels."[17]

Stotsky said the press coverage at the time the report was released missed the real story. "Amazingly, no reporter saw fit to comment on the fact that the decline in literacy skills among college graduates and those with graduate study or degrees . . . was confined to males." Depending on the category of reading, scores for women either stayed flat or rose.

Educators say the biggest shift in reading ability they see is among white boys from blue-collar families. While working on an editorial about the boy troubles, I asked the Southern Regional Education Board (SREB) to conduct a special data run on a unique group of students they track. The data on 40,000 students from 1,000 schools in 26 states targeted the "average" students, those in programs for students most likely headed directly into the workforce, two-year-colleges, technical training programs, or less-competitive four-year colleges. Nearly a third of these boys scored "below basic" in reading skills on the federal National Assessment of Educational Progress tests (compared to 20 percent of the girls). Those reading levels are too low for either college or any job that requires understanding manuals, such as car repair instructions. We're "losing" many average boys, said Gene Bottoms from SREB, who conducted the survey. The poor reading skills arise from school attitude problems picked up in the same survey, said Bottoms: Seven in ten of these "average" girls thought doing well in school was important for achieving life goals, compared to 57 percent of the boys.[18] "These boys see high school as irrelevant."

WHY ISN'T ANYONE SOUNDING THE ALARM?

Actually, the alarms have been sounding for years. In England and Australia, educators have warned the world that the problems they discovered with boys are not unique to their own countries. That warning, however, was never heeded by the U.S. Department of Education.

One of the starkest missed opportunities to learn of the boy troubles arose in 1988, when California educators embarked on a misguided experiment to shift wholesale to "whole language" instruction, where children attempt to pick up reading skills naturally, absent phonics instruction, from reading literature. Not until 1997 did the state reverse course by banning texts that shunned instruction on basic reading techniques. "For too long, teachers have had to secretly sneak phonics-based textbooks into the classroom," said then governor Pete Wilson. By hindsight, academic investigators now pinpoint that shift as the beginning of California's plunge in academic achievement, a remarkable decline documented by PBS correspondent John Merrow in his broadcast "First to Worst."[19] That disastrous decade-long fad was an ideal opportunity to draw some lessons about what happens when boys, who are less adept than girls in picking up literacy skills absent phonics, are deprived of any phonics instruction. Learning those lessons, however, never happened.

The next missed opportunity arose in the mid-1990s, when National Institutes of Health researcher Reid Lyon, who oversaw a reading research program there, warned that tens of thousands of young black boys were being diverted to special education for reading disabilities (a near-certain ticket to dropping out in later grades) that essentially didn't exist. Their teachers simply didn't know how to teach them reading. (As reading expert William Brozo will explain in the next chapter, most girls are wired to get a faster start on reading, but with proper teaching the boys should catch up between fourth and sixth grades. Problem is, with many boys that's not happening.) With the backing of President George W. Bush and prominent Republicans in Congress, Lyon's star rose quickly, culminating in the $1 billion-a-year Reading First program. By 2007, however, the program began collapsing from the weight of abusive management and lackluster evaluations. What had seemed like an ideal opportunity to learn the impact research-based reading programs could have on boys ran aground.

Yet another missed opportunity arose in 2000, when conservative think tanker Christina Hoff Sommers burst onto the scene with her book *The War Against Boys: How Misguided Feminism Is Harming Our Young Men.* Sommers deftly laid out the problems boys were having, but then detoured into gender politics by blaming feminists for the problem, a dubious proposition that even she steers clear of today. Playing the ideological blame game blunted what could have been a timely warning. Over the same time period, book writers such as Michael Gurian, Leonard Sax, Jeffrey Wilhelm, and Michael Smith pointed to male literacy problems and offered corrections, but it was never enough to elevate the issue to the national agenda. For the most part, that left the issue to on-the-ground educators to uncover, one at a time.

The Likely Causes of the
Reading Lapses

ALTHOUGH LITERACY ISSUES appear to head the list of what causes the gender gaps, the reasons behind the literacy lapses are many. Any attempt to rebalance the gender gaps that focuses on just one or two factors will inevitably fall short. The list includes the following causes.

LACK OF PHONICS

Carol Stevens retains an exceptionally clear memory of the phone call she received from her son's fourth grade teacher: "Mrs. Stevens, did you know Steve is having problems reading? Shocked, Carol immediately shot back, "No he's not." I can still remember Carol telling me this story. She and her husband, Erik Brady, worked with me on the startup of *USA Today,* where today he's an award-winning sports reporter. At one point, Carol was editor of the paper's editorial page (which made her my boss). Today, she is managing editor for the news section. Carol, who graduated from Syracuse University with a journalism degree, and Erik, who graduated from Canisius College with a degree in history, are enthusiastic readers and talented writers, attributes they assumed would pass along to their son.

After Carol and Erik had their son tested, they learned the teacher was right. Steve's teachers in Virginia's highly regarded Arlington County schools, from kindergarten through third grade, had been teaching reading by "whole language," a reading method that holds that learning to read is a natural process children can learn from reading actual literature. By immersing children in the excitement of the beauty of literature, they will pick up the meaning and sounds naturally, thus eliminating the plodding instruction of phonics, where sounds are converted to words in a process something akin to a math formula.

The national whole language movement soared in 1987, when California adopted whole language as official state policy. California school districts choosing to purchase textbooks with the phonics approach risked having to pay for them by themselves. The movement spread throughout the country, quickly embraced by teachers who preferred using literature to formulaic phonics. For some children, whole language did indeed work as a natural way to learn reading. But for most children, the rapid shift was a disaster. By 1992 California test scores had dropped to the fifth lowest in the nation on the NAEP (National Assessment of Educational Progress) tests. Not until 1995, when California's reading scores hit the bottom of the nation's rankings, did educators move to re-embrace phonics.

The number of children affected by the plunge into whole language instruction is large but unknowable. The interesting question is the special harm inflicted on boys, who more than girls seem to need the phonics-intense instruction methods recommended in the 2000 National Reading Panel, a two-year research effort by the National Institutes of Health (literacy skills had plunged to the point where they were considered a health problem) to find the most effective reading techniques.

There's a scarcity of research targeting boy/girl differences in absorbing language, but experienced reading experts agree that boys need phonics instruction more than girls. Boys are less adept at intuiting the structure of language, reading expert Louisa Moats explains, which means that teachers need to make it more explicit for them. That's why girls did better with whole language than boys. Agreeing with Moats is Barbara Foorman, one of the nation's top reading experts, who served as the first commissioner of research for the U.S. Department of Education. Explicit reading instruction (the opposite of whole language) helps struggling readers the most, and more boys than girls qualify as struggling readers.

What Carol and Erik learned from the testing experts was that Steve was so bright—already he was working more than a grade level ahead in math—he was able to memorize words. But the lack of phonics instruction left him unable to sound them out, thereby depriving him of the ability to learn new words on his own. Suddenly, a lot of clues that had appeared in the past made sense, such as the times when she was driving Steve and his friends to an event and the friends could sound out the street names they were passing but Steve couldn't. "That was odd, but it didn't ring any bells."

One reason no bells rang was that Carol, at the time, was an unquestioning admirer of the whole language approach to teaching reading. "I loved the idea, introducing kids to great literature, learning the love of language by osmosis." Carol recalls having a discussion about whole language instruction with a friend who taught in an inner-city Baltimore school, the kind of school where an approach other than phonics instruction would amount to instructional malpractice. Carol's friend warned her that whole language doesn't work with all children. "I kind of dismissed that."

Another reason those little clues didn't kick in was because prior to the fourth grade no teacher raised any warning flags about Steve's reading difficulties. "When the subject came up they'd say, 'Oh, don't worry. Boys read later. Besides, boys are stronger in math.' . . . Or, they'd say, 'Boys are more physical. He's going to be more interested in going outside to play soccer.' When Carol took Steve's test results to her local school they were surprised. Because he was bright enough to memorize enough words to earn B-minuses in reading, the school officials never suspected a problem. "When the school saw his IQ numbers, they said 'Oh, he should be getting better grades in reading than a B-minus.' That kind of irked me. It's this crazy problem where if a kid is not functioning two grade levels below his age he doesn't get extra help. If a kid is getting C's but should be getting A's, they're not overly concerned. They're only concerned if he's getting F's when it should be C's."

Carol and Erik found a reading tutor for Steve and ordered a "Hooked on Phonics" package. "Every night, after dinner, we'd spend at least twenty minutes with Steve with these step-by-step drills. Pat, pot, pit . . . and then it gradually got more complicated." Eventually, Steve caught up in reading, was placed in the gifted track in many courses, and graduated with his class from the University of Virginia.

POOR TEACHER EDUCATION

In December 2005, respected reading expert Catherine Snow of Harvard released a book[1] calling for radical reforms in the way would-be teachers are taught how to teach reading. "Ninety-nine percent of the teachers in middle schools and high schools are prepared to teach in their content area, not to teach comprehension in their content area," said Snow.[2] If anything, Snow may have understated the problem. In May 2006 the National Council on Teacher Quality released a study concluding that elementary teachers also lacked the right training to teach reading.[3] The council researchers judged the curriculum based on whether it covered the five basics of reading instruction as laid out by the conclusions of the 2000 National Reading Panel: phonemic awareness,[4] phonics, vocabulary, fluency, and comprehension.

Researchers pored over the textbooks and curriculum of seventy-two randomly selected schools. The bar they set was low—just referencing any of the five elements was sufficient. No attempt was made to determine if those elements were taught thoroughly. Only eleven of the colleges reviewed taught all five of the components, while twenty-three colleges taught none of the five.[5] Some education schools protested that they didn't get credit for recent improvements in their instruction. Other education leaders insisted that quality reading instruction includes far more than those five elements. But the findings on poor reading instruction came as no surprise to local school superintendents, who long ago concluded they had to take on the burden of teaching new teachers how to handle reading instruction.

There appears to be little hope that teachers' colleges will reform themselves. The entire field is a mess, concluded Arthur Levine, former president of Teachers College at Columbia University, in a report released as he departed for a new job.[6] "Teacher education right now is the Dodge City of education: unruly and chaotic. . . . There's a chasm between what goes on in the university and what goes on in the classroom."[7]

As a culprit in the boy problems, it would be hard to overstate the role played by teachers' colleges.

LACK OF READING INSTRUCTION IN THE UPPER GRADES

Only months after graduating from college with an English degree I walked into an upstate New York high school on a one-year assignment to replace a teacher on sabbatical. Armed with a few education courses and practice teaching experience carried out in a small, bucolic Ohio community, I figured I knew plenty to make it through a year of teaching high school. Just how wrong I was struck me on the first day, when I found I had been assigned every functionally illiterate eleventh grader they could round up. As a further reminder of my lowly status as a replacement teacher, I also got assigned restricted study hall duty and the cafeteria watch. Quickly I discovered that learning to break up cafeteria fights was going to be far easier than learning to teach sixteen-year-olds how to read. Even if I could turn my back on the class (not advised) to help a single student, what would I do? Basic reading instruction was never part of my preparation for a secondary teaching certificate.

That was several decades ago, but little has changed. Most educators still view elementary school as the place where reading instruction starts and ends. By middle school, children are expected to make the transition to stiffer content courses. In those grades, literacy becomes, well, something more literate—novels, short stories, poems, writing exercises, the fine points of grammar. Today, we're all paying a price for that attitude. In 2007 the federal NAEP tests revealed that 69 percent of eighth graders fell below the proficient level in their ability to comprehend text at their grade level. Even more worrisome, 26 percent had comprehension below the basic level, which means they had no chance of absorbing the math and science class work.

When Rhode Island educators recently concluded that a fourth of their children read below grade level, the state joined others in discovering that the reading problems, especially with boys, grow through the grades. Some of the largest gender gaps are found in the scores of eleventh graders—the very grade I was teaching in upstate New York. "Nationally, we are seeing 70 percent of entering seventh graders two to three grade levels behind in reading," said Andres Henriquez, a literacy specialist at the Carnegie Foundation, reacting to the Rhode Island discoveries.[8] "We have for many years supported younger children reading, but reading for deeper comprehension is a complex skill set, and we have a dearth of research on what older kids need to learn how to read."

In Providence, where more than half the students read below grade level, educators point to poverty and the influx of immigrants from non-English-speaking countries. But fingering poverty masks a broader problem with boys and reading. As University of Alaska psychologist Judith Kleinfeld found when she looked at the national reading data, this extends well into the middle class. Not until recent years have educators awakened to the threat. Due to inadequate reading skills, nearly a third of all eighth graders are at risk of dropping out of high school, concluded the advocacy group Alliance for Excellent Education in 2006. Students entering ninth grade reading significantly below grade level are twenty times more likely to drop out.

In 2006, Idaho state educators discovered the literacy slippage among their students. Although nearly 90 percent of Idaho third graders scored at top reading levels, that fell to 74 percent in seventh grade and rose only to 77 percent in the tenth grade.[9] To counter the slide, Idaho's state school superintendent announced a plan to push an ongoing elementary literacy program into the upper grades. "We tend to think about literacy as just learning to read, but in the older grades you are reading to learn," said a spokeswoman for the state education department. That same year Tennessee announced a similar plan. "We see that as we pass the fourth grade our reading scores go down and reading isn't emphasized as much as we'd like it to be," said Keith Brewer, Tennessee's deputy education commissioner. "If a child cannot read, they'll be deficient in science, social studies and math."[10]

In 2007 the U.S. Department of Education released a report identifying the "barriers" that prevent middle school students from getting the reading help they need:[11]

> Researchers have found that some teachers circumvent the need for students to read texts by adjusting their assignments or methods of presenting content. . . . Another researcher found that content-area teachers expressed resistance to the work of the high school reading specialists, whose job is to provide students with additional help outside their regular class structure. And still others have suggested that teachers who strive primarily to cover the content of their disciplines are unaware that by increasing students' ability to read their assignments they could actually increase the depth and breadth of content that could be covered efficiently. A final barrier is that when schools actually institute programs to help struggling adolescent readers, they are housed within special education programs and thus serve only a small proportion of the students whom they could benefit.

Allow me to translate: They pass 'em on to the next grade.

INATTENTION TO ROLE MODEL ISSUES

When I met Ken Hilton in 2004 he was a statistician working out of a small cinder-block office in the administration building of the Rush-Henrietta Schools in the suburbs of Rochester, New York, where he oversaw testing and research for this large suburban district. Several years prior to my visit a board member showed up to see his son inducted into the National Honor Society. What he saw was a long line of girls moving across the stage: "I heard nothing but heels clicking," said the board member. Concerned about the obvious gender gap, he asked Hilton what was going on. Hilton couldn't answer, but he vowed to get to the bottom of it. Hilton is a pocket-protector kind of guy who arrived at his half-basement office every Sunday to catch up on work. When he promises results, he delivers. After six years of probing the issue, Hilton produced some of the most interesting (unpublished) research into the gender gap.

To reach his conclusions Hilton conducted a series of studies, culminating in the summer of 2004 with a large survey of twenty-one school districts across New York state. Twelve were blue-collar and middle-class districts just like Rush-Henrietta. Another nine were among the wealthiest school districts in the state. Here is what Hilton found: In the first group, the blue-collar and middle-class schools, girls not only excelled in verbal skills but each year put a little more academic distance between themselves and the boys. Even in math, long thought to be a male stronghold, girls did better. But the real leap for girls was in reading.

Another significant find: In these districts, the big hit boys take in reading happens in middle school as they hit puberty. That's when a modest gap in verbal skills evident in elementary school doubles in size. But why are some boys faring better than others and a few schools managing to level the gender playing field? Hilton's research on the wealthiest schools is revealing. Girls still do better in verbal skills in those districts. But Hilton discovered an important distinction. When the wealthy boys enter middle school, they don't lose ground. And that holds steady through high school.

Why the smaller verbal gender gaps in upper-income families? Hilton can only feel his way on this one, in part by drawing lessons from his own family, which teems with educators. At nights and on weekends, Hilton saw his father reading, just as the boys hitting puberty today in the wealthiest districts see their well-educated fathers reading. If your father reads, it's not viewed as a sissy thing, as it has come to be seen by many blue-collar students. Not only would that explain why the verbal gap doesn't widen for boys in the wealthiest districts, but it would also partly explain why elite universities such as Harvard, Princeton, and Stanford have roughly 50–50 gender balances.

Is Hilton's educated hunch right? We know from high-income school districts such as Wilmette and Edina that boys there are having literacy problems as well. What Hilton accomplished was putting those problems in perspective. While the boys in Wilmette lag behind the girls there, a far sharper gender divide is found in schools serving blue-collar boys. There, boys are far more likely to have dropped to a literacy level that endangers their future.

Hilton was one of the first educators to examine the gender gap. When I caught up with him in the spring of 2009 he had moved on to become superintendent of a rural school district in upstate New York. Little has changed, reported Hilton from his new job. "Yesterday I met with the high school and middle school principals to review tally sheets [student registration data] for next year's classes. In our two advanced placement English classes we'll have twenty-four boys and fifty-seven girls. In AP biology we'll have six boys and twenty-six girls. Next year's AP course with the greatest gender balance is AP calculus, but even there girls will outnumber boys nine to eight. And our district's National Honor Society gender imbalance is a mirror of what I discovered ten years ago at Rush-Henrietta. Two weeks ago we had the annual NHS induction dinner and ceremony. Of the thirty-seven new members, only ten were boys. Boys seem to be underachieving here in the Catskills just like they are elsewhere in America."

LACK OF BOY BOOKS

Melissa Mourges is a fifty-three-year-old lawyer who lives on the North Shore of Long Island. She and her husband, also a lawyer, have two children, a fifteen-year-old daughter and a twelve-year-old son, who both attend Catholic schools:

> My son will not read books about girls, while my daughter will read anything, including plays and poetry. One of my favorite books as a child was *Island of the Blue Dolphins* by Scott O'Dell, a Robinson Crusoe story about a teenage Native American girl left alone to fend for herself on a Pacific island. I was thrilled when it was assigned to my son the summer before fourth grade. Our bedtime reading ritual involved him sitting on my lap as we alternated reading paragraphs out loud. Although the book has cute baby otters, murderous Russians, knife fights, fires, wild dogs who kill a boy, and lots and lots of dolphins, my son was left cold. He said he didn't care what happened to the girl. On the other hand, he was transfixed by *Hatchet* by Gary Paulson. This story involves a young boy marooned in the Canadian wilderness for a year, who faces many of the same challenges described in *Dolphins*.

Overall, however, her daughter's reading consumption overwhelmed her son's, perhaps explaining their school records. While her daughter excels in high school honors courses, her son is languishing in seventh grade, more interested in video games than schoolwork. Given that reading is a key to succeeding in school, how can parents lure their sons into reading? It won't be easy. Here's an exercise anyone can do. Visit your local bookstore and find your way to the adolescent literature section. Skim the titles and decide for yourself whether most of the books are targeting girls. I'll spare you the trip: They are. Actually, that makes good business sense. Publishers are less likely to target groups that don't read and boys aren't reading much. There are some indications of fresh publishing attention directed at boys. *The Dangerous Book for Boys*[12] comes to mind. But there's a lot of gender ground to make up.

Authors who make their way through New York's publishing world say there are other reasons. "It's also the people who work in that business," said Jon Scieszka, a former teacher who founded the lively Guys Read website that offers reading suggestions for boys and men. He is also the author of *The True Story of the 3 Little Pigs* and *The Stinky Cheese Man*. "They're mostly young women and they promote books they really like. To make things worse, many boy-friendly books that get published never make their way into classrooms. A classic example, he said, is the *Captain Underpants* series of books. "This isn't a series of books most teachers would love to promote. It works against their every urge of literacy. They say, 'This can't be literacy.'" One is tempted to sympathize with the teachers. Those not familiar with the wild series may need a refresher on some of the titles. There's *Captain Underpants and the Attack of the Talking Toilet, Captain Underpants and the Invasion of the Incredibly Naughty Cafeteria Ladies from Outer Space, Captain Underpants and the Perilous Plot of Professor Poopypants*, and, finally, *Captain Underpants and the Wrath of the Wicked Wedgie Woman*.[13] Sounds disgusting, but actually these are perfect boy books. Check out the comments from parents on Amazon. Typical: "My son is reading!"

The gender gap in books developed in the 1980s and continues through today, said Anita Silvey, the author of several guides to children's books. The feminist movement of the 1970s produced a gusher of books portraying "strong girls" as protagonists who take charge of whatever challenges they face. The best example is Newbery Award winner *The True Confessions of Charlotte Doyle*,[14] the story of thirteen-year-old Charlotte and her adventures crossing the Atlantic in 1832. The once-prim Charlotte is radically transformed by a mutiny and becomes a swashbuckling crew member who eventually takes command of the ship. Somehow, boys got left out of the girls-can-do movement, with the male protagonist novels aimed at the seven- to twelve-year-old market mostly disappearing, said Silvey. "Novels became the domain of girls."

There's little dispute that boys have fewer books to choose from, said Kristen McLean, executive director of the Association of Booksellers for Children. "If you walk into a bookstore and you're looking for a book for a fourteen-year-old boy you might be able to get some good recommendations but very few book sellers pull a section together just for boys. I think it's because of the perception that girls buy more books and to some degree that's true."

The dearth of boy books is part of a larger trend of publishers aiming at women rather than men. And why shouldn't they? According to the National Endowment for the Humanities reading surveys, reading among men has plummeted. In early 2007, *New York Times* columnist Maureen Dowd wrote about a visit to a Washington bookstore:[15]

> Suddenly I was swimming in pink. I turned frantically from display table to display table, but I couldn't find a novel without a pink cover. I was accosted by a sisterhood of cartoon women, sexy string beans in minis and stilettos, fashionably dashing about book covers with the requisite urban props—lattes, books, purses, shopping bags, guns and, most critically, a diamond ring. Was it a Valentine's Day special?
>
> No, I realized with growing alarm, chick lit was no longer a niche. It had staged a coup of the literature shelves. Hot babes had shimmied in the grizzled old boys' club, the land of Conrad, Faulkner and Maugham.

If Dowd had visited the adolescent readers section she would have seen where that trend starts, with stacks and stacks of books aimed at girls. Publishers find it easier to market to girls, said McLean. "Girls tend to be more comfortable picking out books and they tend to read more. . . . In a way, it's a chicken-and-egg issue."

A paucity of high-quality nonfiction story telling that would appeal to boys is what drove Boston-based publishing veteran Steve Hill to launch his own small publishing company, Flying Point Press. When Hill, the father of two boys, went looking for the kind of adventure, history, and travel books that captivated him as a child, he found that the best books were out of print. Most of the boy-friendly books Hill found were "tepid books by not very good writers." Publishers put out ten girl-oriented books for every boy book, estimates Hill. "I believe most children's publishers believe that boys don't read. And traditionally, most children's publishers are run by women. Most publishers are market-oriented and believe the boy market is smaller. They put their energies into picture books for younger kids and fictions for girls. That's a bigger market." (The observations by Hill and Scieszka about women dominating children's book publishing are not disputed. Although plenty of men are found on the business side of children's publishing, the top editors who choose which books get published are mostly women.)

Hill's Flying Point Press specializes in bringing back to life old titles and underwriting new works by master storytellers. "These books have to be part of a series, so if a boy likes a book about the sinking of the Bismarck and sees another book from the same series about Lawrence of Arabia or D-Day, he'll have confidence these other books are going to be good." Anyone writing for Flying Point has to understand the boy mentality. "Boys are not into feelings, people skills, or personalities. They're very much into things. Tanks and guns and buildings and submarines and airliners. They like to know how things work. They like the details. What kind of gun did Daniel Boone carry with him as he went over the Cumberland Gap? What was his life like? What kind of animals did he shoot?"

Thing-oriented books describes Scieszka's latest project, producing a series of books he hopes will get boys hooked on reading early. "As soon as a kid walks into preschool I want him to find cool books he will want to read." Thus was born *Trucktown*, inspired by memories of his father taking him to see construction sites. "We'd sit there for hours. There's something about little guys and trucks." Despite the setbacks Scieszka has experienced trying to reach boys with reading (described in the concluding chapter), he's optimistic that recent publicity about boys may have changed some minds in the publishing world. Silvey agrees, saying she has started to see publishers reach out for more boy-friendly books.

"Graphic novels are starting to take hold," said Scieszka, "and more teachers and librarians are beginning to see nonfiction books as legitimate reading. Boys tend to like nonfiction, but for years those books were looked down upon in school. The attitude of the teachers was that only a novel was real literature." The *Trucktown* series is one reason Scieszka is hopeful about the future: His proposal went to auction with five publishers—always a good sign for an author. An even better sign that things could turn positive: In 2006 the Library of Congress named Scieszka the first National Ambassador for Young People's Literature.

PUSHING LITERACY ON BOYS TOO SOON

In December 2008, the *Minneapolis Star Tribune* published a story with this headline: "Kids not ready for kindergarten cost Minnesota schools $113 million a year." The reporter proceeded to draw a straight line between the dearth of these "readiness" skills and maladies such as being assigned to special education or dropping out of school. Not once did the writer pause to ask: Wait, isn't school supposed to start in kindergarten? Where are children supposed to pick up these prekindergarten skills? The answer, of course, was preschool. The story illustrates a phenomenon that's had a huge impact on boys. Students really do need to be prepared for kindergarten and they really are at risk of problems in later grades if they're not prepared.

The reason preschools are needed goes back to that 1989 education summit in Charlottesville, Virginia, where the state leaders sensed the gathering storm of international competition and concluded that the winnings in this new global tussle would go to the players with the best educations. While the governors were never crass enough to come out and say that college is the new high school, it was written all over their reform package. The central point of high school became preparation for college. To carry out the governors' goal of preparing every child for this new economic reality, educators have pushed academics earlier and earlier. High quality preschools passing along academic skills, they concluded, were the best path for preparing students for the newly stiffened high school curriculums required for college.

As a veteran editorial writer with a focus on education, I've always agreed with those goals. I've written more pro-preschool editorials than I can keep track of. But when researching this book I found parents and some preschool experts raising good questions about the impact academically oriented preschools were having on boys. The skeptics may have a point. Not a single governor asked this question: What would happen if you pushed reading skills on boys before their brains were ready to absorb the building blocks of language? Yvette Keel can tell you: Some boys shut down. Boys such as her son Allen. When I met Keel she was the vice principal of an elementary school in Hinesville, Georgia. Over her career, she taught high school for ten years, worked as a vice principal of a middle school (where she worked with Michael Gurian to introduce single-gender classes to turn around the gender gap there), and earned a Ph.D. in education administration. Little of that prepared her for what she never saw coming.

Her son, Allen, 13,[16] attended a private, half-day preschool before entering kindergarten. With a summer birthday he was younger than the other children, so when he seemed a little slow picking up the letters of the alphabet they held him back for a second year of preschool. For the most part, that seemed to work well, except for his reading. Allen seemed to resist the attempts by the preschool teacher to push reading readiness skills. "We kept a set of flashcards and at night would go through the alphabet. I noticed that on some days he would rattle them off. But on days he'd rather be doing something else, playing in the backyard or playing with puzzles, when I would hold up the letters he wouldn't get it. I would hold up an 'a' and he would say 'r.'" Kindergarten in Georgia is like kindergarten everywhere. Most students are either readers or have the reading readiness skills needed to take off with the other students. Allen, however, was different. Reading skills came slowly, and his interest in reading was minimal.

In the second grade, the teacher called Keel and said, "Your son can't read." Keel was stunned. "I kept saying that according to the standardized tests he was reading on grade level at the end of first grade. How could he come into second grade and not read?" But she got the message. Says Keel: "At that point I started paying attention." Allen was moved from private to public school, but the reading problems lingered. Despite scoring well on standardized tests, including on reading skills, he remained a disinterested reader. "At home he never picked up books. At night if it was time to go to bed, if he wasn't tired he would pick up a Calvin and Hobbs or a Superhero comic book. Only highly visual books. Over the summer he read two books, autobiographies of wrestlers. It's always been like that. If it's something he really wants to do he'll pick it up. But if it's school stuff and he's not interested, he will fail." In later grades, Allen was diagnosed with test anxiety. And then came the assessment that he had a "processing deficit"—lack of phonemic awareness. Translation: Allen never learned the basics of reading. In the opinion of his educator/mother, that resulted from reading being pushed too hard too early. "Was this because his brain was developing and we were forcing him to do something he was not ready to do? He was shutting down that part of his brain."

A few preschool experts are beginning to agree with Yvette. Linda Flach, who works for Connecticut's Early Childhood Consultation Partnership in a children's mental health clinic just outside New Haven, advises preschools on making their facilities more child-friendly and also takes on special cases, usually boys with seemingly insolvable discipline problems. She agrees with Yale's Walter Gilliam that boys are far more likely to be expelled from preschool. In her experience, those expelled from preschools in her area are almost exclusively boys. "What we're usually dealing with is aggressive behavior. It could be a four-year-old biting, pushing, or throwing temper tantrums. The reason most kids get asked to leave involves safety. You may have children running out of the classroom and there's fear they will run into the street."

But why are so many of these boys having these problems? Flach is a practitioner, not a researcher, so she concedes her observations lack the credibility of a data-driven study. But she worries that the push for early academics is hurting the boys. "In my opinion we have a stress factor going on with children. There's a pushdown of academics into preschools. I've seen teachers of two-year-olds sitting there doing lessons on 'This is the color blue.' Sometimes it looks like a didactic lesson for two-year-olds. I'm trying to get across to people that you can't do this with two-year-olds. But it's happening." Preschool, says Flach, should be a time reserved for developing social and emotional attachments, mastering self-control, and learning to get along with others. "People need to get away from thinking that the goal of preschool is to teach them to read and count and add and subtract."

Girls, who mature faster in language development, have the upper hand in any preschool emphasizing verbal skills development. "The worry is that children are learning to hate learning." From birth to five, said Flach, boys have a strong need for movement and outdoor play. "Sometimes I'll visit a program where the children arrive at 7 A.M. to 8 A.M. and the first play time might not be until 11 A.M. These boys come in, sit down, eat breakfast, and they're bursting with energy. If confined to the classroom they may get into negative behaviors."

Agreeing with Flach about the danger of pushing academic skills too early with boys, especially reading, is Larry Griffin, an education training consultant with Kaplan Early Learning Co. "We believe that just because everyone says that children need to read by three does not mean that it should happen by then. We parade a kid out who learned to read before four and say that because he learned to do it, all children should do it." As with other preschool experts who raised the issue of academically oriented preschools doing more harm than good for boys, what he sees worries him. "When the boys walk into the classroom they hear 'talk, talk, talk, read, read, read, write, write write.' Boys are not hardwired to do that from the get-go. In language skills, they lag behind the girls by a year or a year and a half." Asking a boy to sit still and absorb a language lesson is unrealistic, said Griffin. "Boys can learn letters, but they're not going to sit there and trace letters all day like the girls might. They will break the pencil. If you have Play-Doh, though, they will make letters."

Watching teachers call children into story time often makes Griffin wince. "You can see the circle divide into three groups. The first group of children sits up front near the teacher and are really engaged in the experience because they can see the book. Then there's the next layer of kids, I call them middle earth, and they're falling over the first group trying to get closer. Then there's what I call the hinterland group. Those are the kids who are abandoning the group. The strays. And the teacher assistant is constantly rounding up the strays but no sooner do they rejoin the circle than other kids are gone. By far, the majority of those kids are boys."

How much of the gender gaps can be traced back to pushing reading too soon? Considering that preschool is a relatively recent education reform, probably not that much. The greater concern is the possibility that this could become a pro-boys reform destined to backfire.

FAILURE TO TEACH READING PROPERLY

At the outset here, let's get two things straight. First, teaching reading *is* rocket science, which is the title of a great monograph written by reading expert Louisa Moats.[17] Second, I'm not going to pretend that I'm a reading expert and lay out a fifteen-point action plan for teachers and parents. I'll leave that to the reading science experts such as Moats and William Brozo, co-author of a new book published by the International Reading Association on encouraging boy readers.[18]

Moats's report starts out with two premises, that we have a problem and there is a way out. Her description of the problem:

- About 20 percent of elementary students have significant reading problems.

- At least 20 percent of elementary students do not read fluently enough to enjoy or engage in independent reading.

- The rate of reading failure for African-American, Hispanic, and limited-English speakers and poor children ranges as high as 70 percent.

- A third of poor readers nationwide are from college-educated families.

- One of four adults in the United States lacks the basic literacy skills required in a typical job.

Nearly all children can learn to read, writes Moats, but few receive the kind of research-based reading instruction needed to make that happen. The news only gets worse for boy readers, whom Brozo targets. As any parent or teacher can attest, boys are slower to pick up language skills, a phenomenon documented in magnetic resonance imaging, which shows that girls have 11 percent more neurons in the brain areas devoted to language. Those scans show that the language areas of brains in three-and-a-half-year-old girls mirror those of five-year-old boys. It's not that all girls will always turn out to be better readers, cautions Brozo, but on average, they will almost certainly get a faster start. No surprise, then, that girls have adapted nicely to the stiff curriculum pushed down through the grades.

Here's the catch, though, Brozo told me in a phone interview. With the proper support from home and intelligent teaching methods, the typical boy should catch up with the girls between fourth and sixth grades. Currently, that's not happening. In fact, the literacy gaps build through the grades, reaching their strongest differences late in high school, just as students are considering college. So how would this boy-friendly literacy instruction work? Brozo lays out tips ranging from finding the right entry-level book (and not just nonfiction) and offers specific books that celebrate "positive male values," which he defines as cooperation, courage, generosity, honesty, perseverance, respectfulness, responsibility, and tolerance. He offers suggestions on combining play and literacy, although some classroom teachers may gasp at the authors' openness to seeing objects sail through the air:

> The eyes of boys are wired to detect location, direction, and speed, so boys are more likely to draw more active pictures or verbs. Walk into any classroom and it is likely you will see girls drawing rainbows, houses and families and boys drawing spaceships flying through the air. . . . We often hear teachers say that it is typically the boys in a classroom who get into trouble for throwing things. Pencils, crayons, and wads of paper become projectiles that boys toss around, simply to determine where they will land or how fast and far they can go. . . .
>
> [T]he enjoyment boys receive from tossing objects and watching them sail through the air may be used, if it is used carefully. Incorporating soft objects to toss and movement into literacy can enhance the literacy skills of boys, from learning letter sounds to developing fluency. [Brozo then lays out a classroom exercise to demonstrate.]

Are these "boy" traits passed through the genes or learned from society? That's a nice discussion for sociologists, but in the real world of a first grade classroom that matters little.

> Whether one believes that boys and girls think differently because their brains are different, or because of societal expectations, it is undeniable that children act and think differently from adults. These differences are real and teachers must cope with them every day.

Brozo's book is ideal as a guide for teachers and parents who are focusing on a single boy or a classroom of boys, but what about the public policy implications of having so many boys slip behind in school because the reading instruction served up in preschool and the early grades is backfiring? What had appeared to be the "solution" to the problem, the $1 billion-a-year Reading First program that used grant money to lure school districts into using a sophisticated sequence of phonics instruction—a technique that should have bailed out thousands of boys—was officially declared ineffective in 2008. "There was no statistically significant impact on reading comprehension scores in grades one, two or three," Grover J. "Russ" Whitehurst, director of the Institute of Education Sciences, the Education Department's research arm, said in a briefing with reporters. He said students in both groups made gains. "It's possible that, in implementing Reading First, there is a greater emphasis on decoding skills and not enough emphasis, or maybe not correctly structured emphasis, on reading comprehension," he said. "It's one possibility."[19]

That's more than possible, according to E. D. Hirsch, one of the country's best-known education reformers and reading comprehension experts. Hirsch, the former University of Virginia professor who authored *Cultural Literacy,* launched a highly regarded school curriculum reform called Core Knowledge, which delivers an astonishingly rich curriculum to students.[20] Hundreds of Core Knowledge schools, most of them highly successful, give lie to the notion that teaching children *how* to learn matters far more than *what* is taught. In fact, Hirsch argues, children need a rich stew of material to learn to comprehend what they're reading, the exact skill Whitehurst found lacking in the technique-oriented Reading First program.

Hirsch is not someone content with being a critic. In August 2008 New York City schools chancellor Joel Klein announced the city would embark on a ten-school reading experiment designed with Hirsch and the Core Knowledge staff. The purpose, he said, was to erase the "knowledge deficit" city students were revealing on tests. The three-year experiment will track one thousand students using materials from the newly designed Core Knowledge Early Literacy Project. That program will fuse synthetic phonics—an advanced form of phonics thought to be especially helpful with boys, where sounds are blended to make words—with the rich Core Knowledge curriculum.

In a series of e-mail exchanges, Core Knowledge reading expert Matthew Davis explained their approach:

The Core Knowledge Reading program makes a systematic attempt to build cultural literacy and background knowledge, and so does not limit itself to fiction and poetry. It contains fiction and poetry, to be sure. But it also contains a great deal of historical and scientific content, as well as some art and music—all drawn from the Core Knowledge Sequence.

The Core Knowledge Reading program for the early grades (K–2, the ones we are working on now) relies much more heavily on teacher-presented read-alouds than other programs. This is because a typical student's reading comprehension ability does not catch up to his or her listening comprehension ability until middle school. Thus, the most effective channel for learning in these early years, while students are still learning to decode and then building fluency and automaticity, is the ear, not the eye. About one hour a day in our early grades program is devoted to what we call "The Listening and Learning Strand." Every day the students listen to a read-aloud—a fictional story like Casey Jones or a nonfiction piece on the Pilgrims or astronomy, or whatever it might be. Then they discuss.

We have an excellent set of decodable readers (readers with spellings the children already know), with a new story each day. On the day that /ou/ spelled 'ou' is taught, the kids get a story with several examples of /ou/ spelled 'ou' in their reader story. So the readers reinforce the phonics lessons.

It would be gratifying to report that a solution to boys' reading difficulties lies in an already proven experiment or program. Unfortunately, however, educators are still struggling with the problem, with experiments such as the Core Knowledge Early Literacy Project holding out the most promise.

C H A P T E R

The Writing Failures

IN THE SPRING of 2009, Annmarie Neal, a psychologist who works at Cisco Systems to develop upper-management talent, accompanied her child's class of five-year-olds to the Denver Art Museum to see an exhibit on samurai warriors. Once at the museum, the girls sat together peacefully and asked polite questions of the museum's monitor. The boys, by contrast, wanted to touch everything everywhere and their questions were often impolitely blurted out. Especially noticeable was one little boy who hopped up and down on one foot while asking questions. The teacher advised the boy to sit down, gather his thoughts carefully—and then ask a question.

The squirmy boy reminded Neal of some of the employees she advises at Cisco. Last September in Singapore, for example, she oversaw a meeting of Cisco's Action Learning Forum, a team ranging from newly promoted distinguished engineers to top business leaders, all boring in on a complex business problem. One particular engineer stood out. He had terrible presentation skills; his grammar was askew, his thoughts nonlinear. As a result, he was ignored by the rest of the group. Problem was, he had some of the best ideas.

Too many employees, says Neal, arrive at companies such as Cisco with great technical expertise but abysmal abilities to communicate, especially in writing. Once they move away from the safety net of spell-check/grammar-check, they risk embarrassing themselves, and their great ideas get ignored. Just like that five-year-old in the Denver Art Museum.

In 2009 Neal contributed a chapter on communication lapses for the book *The Global Achievement Gap*.[1] "We see folks who don't know how to spell, how to complete a sentence that's grammatically correct. It's a huge issue for us." Those lapses are overlooked in both K–12 schools and college. The problem is especially obvious among the predominantly male software engineers.

Neal suspects it has something to do with what she saw in the museum that day. From that boy's perspective, he was told his thoughts were not worthy because he could not contain his squirminess. "School systems can overlook and not foster development in little people like that, and that's not good. You could be looking at a pattern that develops over ten years." If the boy concludes he has great thoughts but knows he has trouble sitting still, he'll be okay. But if he concludes he can't have great thoughts because he can't sit still—that's another boy lost in the system who will never absorb all the skills schools should be passing along, especially communication skills he may not think he needs, she said.

The signs of the gender writing gaps spill out everywhere. In August 2006 newspapers across the country treated the results of the new SAT test as Page One news. It was the first time a writing segment—which would count a full third of the total score—was added to the famous test. Most newspapers led with the College Board's announcement of unprecedented drops in scores, the biggest annual drop in reading scores in thirty-one years. But that wasn't the real story. Only education writer Jay Mathews of the *Washington Post* and a few other reporters divined the real story, which was that girls, once again, were coming out on top. By boosting the SAT scoring by a third on writing skills alone, the College Board was handing a gift to girls, who are far better writers than boys. Sure enough, girls outscored boys by eleven points. No surprise there. Girls have always scored better than boys on national writing tests. Unfortunately for the boys, however, their writing skills are slipping.[2] In fact, writing is the one area where the gender gap is roughly the same as the racial gap. That revelation tends to surprise educators, who assume that racial gaps always outweigh gender gaps.

The gender gaps in writing tend to surprise even the experts. In the spring of 2008 the National Assessment Governing Board released the 2007 NAEP (National Assessment of Educational Progress) writing results, leaving Amanda Avallone, the vice chair of the group, aghast. Avallone, an eighth grade English teacher and assistant principal in Boulder, Colorado, released this statement:

> The gender gap in writing is almost as wide as the racial/ethnic differences, and much greater than it is in science and math. In 12th-grade writing, 32 percent of female students have reached Proficient, which is double the 16 percent of males at or above that achievement level. . . . If writing well is vital for all, then we cannot be satisfied until all are achieving at a high level. Based on my classroom experiences, the gap between boys and girls, especially at grade 8—the level I teach—troubles and mystifies me. According to the new NAEP report card, 43 percent of girls reach the Proficient level for 8th grade, compared to just 22 percent of boys. Though I am not an expert on gender differences, I have been a teacher and observer of boys and girls as writers throughout my career. Nothing in my experience tells me that boys cannot write. Just like girls, they love words—what they mean, how they sound, what they feel like on the tongue and in the mind. They enjoy stringing words together to share their knowledge and expertise and, above all, to construct an argument. I've also observed equal aptitude for mastering grammar and developing voice. Over the years, boys have been as likely as girls to tell me—quietly, after class—of the stories, poems, and songs they create outside of school.
>
> Why, then, do indicators of writing ability like the NAEP assessment consistently report that male students are not achieving at the same level as their female counterparts? I cannot answer this question definitively, but I do suspect that the gender gap is in part the result of lower expectations for boys in the area of literacy, writing in particular. These days, I seldom if ever hear the message that math and science do not matter for girls. Yet, I do still encounter the myth that many boys won't really need to write very much or very well once they leave school.

She's right. Boys with limited writing skills have no idea what is awaiting them in college, where regardless of their major they must get through English 101. Even science and math majors have to express their thoughts in narrative form. In 2008 the College Board released data showing that its writing test is a better predictor of grades for college freshmen than the older, more familiar SAT test. That's not just a matter of the College Board promoting its own test. The University of California reached the same conclusion.[3]

Some discount the gender gaps in writing as a natural breakdown between girls and boys. Girls are better writers; boys are better at math and science, right? Actually, on a lot of recent state tests girls have topped boys in math while pulling far ahead on literacy skills. On the federal NAEP test, boys enjoy a modest advantage in science and math but get tromped by the girls in reading. Here are the numbers:

- In writing, 32% of females score proficient or above, compared to 16% of the boys. In reading, 41% of the females are proficient, compared to 29% of males.

- In science, 16% of girls are proficient, compared to 21% of males. In math, 21% of females are proficient, compared to 25% of the males.

Avallone shouldn't have been so surprised. The fact that American students have writing problems is not new. The National Commission on Writing released a study in 2003 with these findings:[4]

- Most fourth grade students spend less than three hours a week writing. That's 15% of the time they spend watching TV.

- Nearly two out of every three high school seniors do not write a three-page paper for their English teachers as often as once a month.

■   Three out of every four seniors never receive writing assignments in history or social studies.

Interestingly, that study didn't break out the research by gender, a common practice that masks gender gaps. If it had, commission researchers would have discovered that the bulk of the writing problems lie with boys, just as the National Assessment of Educational Progress has documented. National writing tests released that same year found that 40 percent of eighth grade girls scored as proficient writers, compared to only 20 percent of boys.[5]

The gender gaps in writing appear to connect directly to the gaps in reading. "Can anyone learn to write at all without also knowing how to read?" asked English professor Milton Freedman[6] in an op-ed pointing out the connection. "Simply, literacy includes capacity to read." Too many teachers separate the functions, said Freedman. "Some often teach writing in a vacuum empty of reading. They mainly use multiple-choice tests to find out what details in a novel, play, or poem students recall or which misspellings they recognize, not whether they have grasped nuances of characters or plot."

Teachers also appear to assume that boys will always be inferior writers. Just a matter of boys being boys. And that attitude has seeped down to the students. "Students themselves don't feel boys are as capable as girls are in writing," concluded University of Toronto professor Shelley Peterson, who asked four hundred Ohio students in grades four, six, and eight to review writing samples written by students in a neighboring district. The students, who came from urban, suburban, and rural districts, were asked to identify the gender of the authors. If the stories were descriptive and well written, the students assumed the writers were female. If the stories had spelling errors and poor grammar, it was assumed the authors were boys.[7] "Children often live up to the expectations of adults," said Peterson. "If boys view themselves to be poorer writers, they will give the impression that they are poorer writers. This can impact their decision to have any career which involves writing."

ANSWERS FROM A WRITING COACH: RALPH FLETCHER

"I think over time the voice in boys writing—their humor, energy, passion—tends to disappear because it is not being encouraged in school," said writing instructor Ralph Fletcher in an interview.[8] "Rather, many teachers perceive boy writers as a problem to be managed. No wonder their voice gets dimmed and finally extinguished." Fletcher has an interesting perspective on the boy writing problems. Despite devoting his career to writing workshops, he confesses he was late to realize that writing skills among boys were slipping. When Fletcher realized he had missed something, he made amends by researching a book on the problem, *Boy Writers*.[9] "I observed most boys dutifully putting pencil to the paper, but many seemed to be merely going through the motions. . . . A few of the guys were writing with gusto, but the general demeanor of those boys troubled me." Fletcher listed the symptoms among boys: turned off, checked out, disengaged, disenfranchised. The condition of boys and writing had sunk to the level of "failure to thrive," says Fletcher, referring to the syndrome of troubled babies failing to gain weight.

Fletcher cites the national data on writing, where high school senior boys lag far behind the girls. But he also points to state writing tests, where the gaps are equally dramatic. In Washington state, for example, girls at all grade levels outscore boys by eighteen points. "When I looked at other states I found the same thing—girls trouncing boys on the state writing tests." So where's the problem? First there's the matter of handwriting. It's no secret that young boys lack the motor skills to execute fine handwriting. "Does boys' poor handwriting negatively affect the way teachers respond to their writing?" asks Fletcher. "Let's consider a similar question: Do adults lavish more positive attention, praise, or higher grades on a child who is more physically attractive than a less attractive child? No parent or teacher would be eager to admit this, yet several classroom studies have confirmed that this is true."

Poor handwriting is just the beginning of what teachers often find dismaying about boys' writing. What boys choose to write about can be gross, violent, or equal parts of both. Here is where the big changes have occurred. Over the past fifteen years, two seemingly unrelated forces—school-based antiviolence campaigns and feminization of the teaching force—have triggered a censorship campaign that deprives some boys of their natural writing material. When Fletcher surveyed teachers to find out what boys liked to write about, the list that came back looked like this: aliens, monsters, horror stories, war, drugs, war-related hero stories, accidents, injuries, thugs, and mistakenly hurting something else. And we can't forget a particular favorite: robots fighting evil characters.

Fletcher said he asked one female fifth grade teacher how she handled the violent topics. "I don't allow blood and guts, so I don't have that problem." Boys, of course, have plenty of non-gory boy topics to write about, ranging from sports to cars to spaceships. But ruling out spaceships locked in intergalactic battles eliminates many things a fourth grade boy wants to write about.

Although these censoring forces were well under way before the 1999 Columbine tragedy, that incident sealed the deal. After Columbine, zero-tolerance attitudes toward violence in writing became common, especially among female teachers. Fletcher draws on the research of Thomas Newkirk, author of *Misreading Masculinity*,[10] who examined how schools reacted to the Columbine tragedy. Columbine was blamed on the impact violent television shows and video games were having on young boys, says Newkirk. "In response, cartoonists depicted boys sitting before their televisions and video screens with wires running to their heads programmed for violence." Boys were depicted as prone to violence and in need of censorship. That prompted many schools to prohibit any violence in writing—akin to what the fifth grade teacher told Fletcher. Teachers encountering violent writing routinely contacted not only school counselors but the parents as well. Writes Newkirk: "Not only is this writing banned from the school, it becomes a potential index of psychological dysfunction, requiring the assistance of a counselor."

While the reaction to Columbine was understandable, we now know that violent video games had nothing to do with that violence.[11] In fact, children can distinguish between fantasy and reality, says Newkirk. In his book, he cites the development of *Sesame Street*.[12] At first, the show developers followed the advice of psychologists who warned against mixing real and fantasy characters, such as having Big Bird talk to Maria. That would only confuse children, they were told. But children didn't like the show. "Finally, in desperation the developers decided to reject this advice, to mix the fantasy and human characters. The rest, as they say, is history. Children had no problem with the mixture." Another flaw in the logic, says Newkirk, is a presumed solid link between fantasy violence and real-world violence. Japanese children consume heavy doses of violent programming. The *Mighty Morphin Power Rangers*, for example, was a Japanese import. The newer cartoons from Japan are even more violent. "According to the 'effects' research, if this is the standard fare for Japanese children, one would expect that there would be a major problem of violence in Japanese society—yet the crime rate is one of the world's lowest."

Depriving boys of the option of writing about violence saps their motivation to write, argue both Fletcher and Newkirk. In *Misreading Masculinity*, Newkirk cites a conversation with one fourth grader he calls Ethan: "You need violence to have an adventure. And you need some death to have an adventure story—for the main character to go out and have a reason to go out, like a big journey or something." Not only are boys denied the writing themes of fright and violence, they are often discouraged from writing about what teachers see as socially unredeeming topics, says Newkirk. Professional wrestling, for example, is another favorite writing subject for boys.

But is professional wrestling as unredeeming as it might seem to a female fourth grade teacher? Its gaudiness, violence, and assault on political correctness make it an easy target. It's hard to imagine professional wrestling as an agent for creating better world citizens, concedes Newkirk. But that doesn't make wrestling an unsuitable topic. Wrestling, says Newkirk, "turns the world upside down, mocking those in authority (teachers, judges, politicians, parents, referees) whose job it is to monitor and evaluate our behavior." As such, writing or reading about professional wrestling becomes a vehicle for parody and satire, the elements at work in many great works of literature. The point made by both Newkirk and Fletcher is not to extol topics such as wrestling or violence but rather to expand the notion of what's considered acceptable writing material.

Later in the book I will describe the success I saw Maryland educators have with comic books and graphic novels. Newkirk and Fletcher have it right. The alternative—boring boys to death by restricting their reading and writing—isn't working. Writes Newkirk, "My main worry is about boys who are alienated from school itself, who find the reading and writing in schools unrelated to anything that matters to them. Such boys— and I was one of them—partition their lives into 'schoolwork' and 'things that really matter.' For some, parental pressure and expectations are enough to keep them at it; others simply disengage. I worry about them. And there are a lot of them out there."

BUT WHAT ABOUT ONLINE READING AND WRITING?

In September 2008, one of my favorite thinkers on the subject of literacy, Emory University professor Mark Bauerlein, wrote a commentary for *The Chronicle of Higher Education* with the title "Online Literacy Is a Lesser Kind." Here's the top third of Bauerlein's piece:

> When Jakob Nielsen, a Web researcher, tested 232 people for how
> they read pages on screens, a curious disposition emerged. Dubbed
> by *The New York Times* "the guru of Web page 'usability,'" Nielsen
> has gauged user habits and screen experiences for years, charting
> people's online navigations and aims, using eye-tracking tools to map
> how vision moves and rests. In this study, he found that people took
> in hundreds of pages "in a pattern that's very different from what
> you learned in school." It looks like a capital letter F. At the top,
> users read all the way across, but as they proceed their descent quick-

ens and horizontal sight contracts, with a slowdown around the middle of the page. Near the bottom, eyes move almost vertically, the lower-right corner of the page largely ignored. It happens quickly, too. "F for fast," Nielsen wrote in a column. "That's how users read your precious content."

The F-pattern isn't the only odd feature of online reading that Nielsen has uncovered in studies conducted through the consulting business Nielsen Norman Group (Donald A. Norman is a cognitive scientist who came from Apple; Nielsen was at Sun Microsystems). A decade ago, he issued an "alert" entitled "How Users Read on the Web." It opened bluntly: "They don't."

In the eye-tracking test, only one in six subjects read Web pages linearly, sentence by sentence. The rest jumped around chasing keywords, bullet points, visuals, and color and typeface variations. In another experiment on how people read e-newsletters, informational e-mail messages, and news feeds, Nielsen exclaimed, "'Reading' is not even the right word." The subjects usually read only the first two words in headlines, and they ignored the introductory sections. They wanted the "nut" and nothing else. A 2003 Nielsen warning asserted that a PDF file strikes users as a "content blob," and they won't read it unless they print it out. A "booklike" page on screen, it seems, turns them off and sends them away. Another Nielsen test found that teenagers skip through the Web even faster than adults do, but with a lower success rate for completing tasks online (55 percent compared to 66 percent). Nielsen writes: "Teens have a short attention span and want to be stimulated. That's also why they leave sites that are difficult to figure out." For them, the Web isn't a place for reading and study and knowledge. It spells the opposite. "Teenagers don't like to read a lot on the Web. They get enough of that at school."

Those and other trials by Nielsen amount to an important research project that helps explain one of the great disappointments of education in our time. I mean the huge investment schools have made in technology, and the meager returns such funds have earned.

Ever since the Telecommunications Act of 1996, money has poured into public-school classrooms. At the same time, colleges have raced to out-technologize one another. But while enthusiasm swells, e-bills are passed, smart classrooms multiply, and students cheer—the results keep coming back negative. When the Texas Education Agency evaluated its Technology Immersion Pilot, a $14-million program to install wireless tools in middle schools, the conclusion was unequivocal: "There were no statistically significant effects of immersion in the first year on either reading or mathematics achievement." When University of Chicago economists evaluated California schools before and after federal technology subsidies (the E-Rate program) had granted 30 percent more schools in the state Internet access, they determined that "the additional investments in technology generated by E-Rate had no immediate impact on measured student outcomes." In March 2007, the National Center for Education Evaluation and Regional Assistance evaluated 16 award-winning education technologies and found that "test scores were not significantly higher in classrooms using selected reading and mathematics software products." Last spring a New York State school district decided to drop its laptop program after years of offering it. The school-board president announced why: "After seven years, there was literally no evidence it had any impact on student achievement—none."

Those conclusions apply to middle-school and high-school programs, not to higher education (which has yet to produce any similarly large-scale evaluations). Nevertheless, the results bear consideration by those pushing for more e-learning on campuses.

Backers, providers, and fans of new technology explain the disappointing measures as a matter of circumstance. Teachers didn't get enough training, they say, or schoolwide coordination was spotty, parents not sufficiently involved. Maybe so, to some extent, but Nielsen's studies indicate another source. Digitized classrooms don't come through for an off-campus reason, a factor largely overlooked by educators. When they add laptops to classes and equip kids with on-campus digital tools, they add something else, too: the reading habits kids have developed after thousands of hours with those same tools in leisure time.

To teachers and professors, a row of glistening new laptops in their classroom after a dozen years with nothing but chalk and blackboard, or a podium that has been transformed from a wooden stand into a multimedia console, can appear a stunning conversion. But to the average freshman walking through the door and finding a seat, it's nothing new. Our students have worked and played with computers for years. The Horatio Alger Association found that students in high school use the Internet four and a half hours per week for help with homework (The State of Our Nation's Youth, 2008–2009), while the National School Boards Association measures social networking at nine hours per week, much of it spent on homework help. The gap between viewpoints is huge. Educators envision a whole new pedagogy with the tools, but students see only the chance to extend long-established postures toward the screen. If digitized classrooms did pose strong, novel intellectual challenges to students, we should see some pushback on their part, but few of them complain about having to learn in new ways.

Once again, this is not so much about the content students prefer—Facebook, YouTube, etc.—or whether they use the Web for homework or not. It is about the reading styles they employ. They race across the surface, dicing language and ideas into bullets and graphics, seeking what they already want and shunning the rest. They convert history, philosophy, literature, civics, and fine art into information, material to retrieve and pass along.

That's the drift of screen reading. Yes, it's a kind of literacy, but it breaks down in the face of a dense argument, a Modernist poem, a long political tract, and other texts that require steady focus and linear attention—in a word, slow reading. Fast scanning doesn't foster flexible minds that can adapt to all kinds of texts, and it doesn't translate into academic reading. If it did, then in a 2006 *Chronicle* survey of college professors, fully 41 percent wouldn't have labeled students "not well prepared" in reading (48 percent rated them "somewhat well prepared"). We would not find that the percentage of college graduates who reached "proficiency" literacy in 1992 was 40 percent, while in 2003 only 31 percent scored "proficient." We would see reading scores inching upward, instead of seeing, for instance, that the percentage of high-school students who reached proficiency dropped from 40 percent to 35 percent from 1992 to 2005.

The online world inhabited by our children does little to lessen the demand for literacy skills while doing much to diminish those skills. The abilities to read challenging texts quickly and write incisive papers based on the reading are the essence of college. And that makes writing a roadblock to either getting into college or graduating with a degree. During my visit to the California State University at Fullerton, where entering freshman girls are far more likely than their male counterparts to graduate within six years,[13] professors cited writing as a key ingredient explaining the differences in performance.

In 2005 a study by the college admissions testing firm ACT revealed that a third of high school students planning on attending college fall short of the basics needed to survive in a college-level English composition course, a requirement for all students. Once again, the study did not attempt to separate the genders, but other studies make it clear that most of those offenders are young men. Vartan Gregorian, president of the Carnegie Corporation, views writing as "tantamount to a survival skill."[14] Referring to the writing problems revealed in a "Writing Next" report (yet another report that failed to separate data by gender), Gregorian said, "In an age of globalization, when economies sink or swim on their ability to mine and manage knowledge . . . we cannot afford to let this generation of ours, or indeed, any other, fall behind the learning curve."

The report from Carnegie laid out the practical problems behind the slippage in writing skills. About one in three government and private-sector workers require on-the-job training in basic writing, according to the study, with private companies spending an estimated $3.1 billion annually on writing remediation. What most educators, parents, and think tank writers continue to miss, though, is the significance of the declining writing skills among boys. Take that SAT as just one example. By shifting a full third of this all-important test to writing, an area where girls consistently outperform the boys, the entire education landscape just became a little less boy-friendly.

CHAPTER

The Blame Game: What Gets Blamed (Unfairly) for the Gender Gaps

THE SEARCH FOR the causes of the boy troubles is littered with false leads, starting with Christina Hoff Sommers's book *The War Against Boys: How Misguided Feminism Is Harming Our Young Men.*[1] Published in 2000, Sommers's book was prescient in warning us that boys, not girls, were the ones struggling in school. The blame, said Sommers, lies with the feminist-dominated teaching profession for designing classroom environments more suited for girls than boys. With the benefit of hindsight it appears that while Sommers was dead-on right about warning that boys were in trouble, she was wrong to pin the blame on feminists. The proof of this is straightforward: The boys' problems are unfolding in many countries, including in cultures where feminist movements have yet to materialize. Dispatching with the blame-the-feminists theory, however, is only a baby step in dealing with the multiple theories put forward to explain the slump in boys' academic ambitions. This task of examining the theories one by one is important. If the malady is misdiagnosed, the cure will remain elusive. I argue that that's exactly what's playing out with the gender gaps. Therefore, it is important to sift through the most commonly cited reasons for the gender gaps, starting with the juiciest of all, video games.

MY BOY IS FOREVER LOST TO VIDEO GAMES!

Three weeks before the 2008 election, when the Barack Obama campaign concluded it needed to reach young males ages 18 to 30, campaign operatives knew exactly where to go: video games. Eighteen video games, including "Guitar Hero" and "Madden 09," were embedded with in-game ads for the campaigns. The political ads, appearing on billboards and elsewhere in the games, reminded players to register for early voting. That smart move must have seemed jarring to those inclined to believe that video games lie at the heart of the gender gaps. Those miscreants actually vote?

These attitudes are understandable. Anyone seeking to pin the blame for the gaps on video games is not lacking for evidence. Consider the arrival of the new Sony PlayStation 3. As eager buyers lined up a day or more in advance outside the stores (all guys in the newspaper photos, naturally), mayhem broke out.[2] Outside a Wal-Mart in West Bend, Wisconsin, a nineteen-year-old man was injured when he ran into a pole while racing with a mob of people lunging for one of the few available spots in line. In Palmdale, California, authorities had to shut down a Super Wal-Mart after desperate buyers got rowdy. Only days later Nintendo offered its Wii for sale, which quickly sold out. Thousands of buyers waited in overnight lines. The first buyer in line at the Toys "R" Us store in Times Square was Isaiah Triforce Johnson, who had been waiting in line for more than a week outfitted with a Nintendo Power Glove, a wearable game controller. Johnson told a reporter he had changed his name in deference to Nintendo's "Zelda" series of games.[3]

The dual frenzies to buy the new PlayStations and Nintendos only confirmed what parents and teachers say to one another: Video games have robbed our boys of academic ambitions, rendering them reclusive, social cripples. Surely any doubt of that fact was erased with the spring 2008 release of *The Dumbest Generation*, by Emory University professor Mark Bauerlein.[4] There's an obvious reason why so many teens can't place the Civil War in a particular century, argues Bauerlein: video games. Not just games, of course, but the entire bandwidth of evils, from texting to social networking via the Internet.

For those who want everything documented in numbers, a 2005 report from the Kaiser Family Foundation laid it out in great detail.[5] Young people are so awash in electronic media that they survive only by multitasking, as in instant messaging their friends while on the cell phone while listening to their iPods. Compared to five years earlier, when Kaiser had done a similar survey, the time spent on video games and computers more than doubled. It doesn't take a researcher to tell you who's playing the elaborate, warlike video games: boys, who often turn into college students with their gaming addictions intact. Some colleges even rearrange their dorm configurations in an attempt to flush more male gamers out into the open to interact with other students.

If you take the love for video games and stir in traditional male college vices of beer guzzling and *SportsCenter* watching, you arrive at what some college administrators dub the Bart Simpson syndrome. One survey of 47,000 college students found that 13 percent confessed that gaming had significantly hindered their academic performance (compared to 8 percent who said alcohol had affected their grades).[6]

The Center for Internet Addiction Recovery lists these among the questions young gamers need to ask themselves:

- Do you need to play online games with increasing amounts of time in order to achieve the desired excitement?

- Are you preoccupied with gaming (thinking about it when offline, anticipating your next online session)?

- Have you lied to friends and family members to conceal the extent of your online gaming?

While psychologists continue to debate what kind of name to slap on video addiction, the game that surfaces when the discussion turns to severe addictions is "World of Warcraft," a fantasy war game shared among millions of players around the world who happily pay a monthly subscription fee to stay in the game. Serious "World of Warcraft" aficionados would have to answer yes to those and other addiction questions. Diane Fisher, a Ph.D. clinical psychologist who was a key member of the team that investigated the boy problems at Wilmette Public Schools, worried that one of her sons might become addicted. "When he was young my son was a great reader. He was very engaged. By fifth grade he kept reading but his reading changed. What really engaged his imagination were more and more elaborate strategy games. . . . I have heard of fifth and sixth grade boys playing 'World of Warcraft' until four in the morning. 'World of Warcraft' is a world these boys live in," said Fisher, who along with her surgeon husband tried gaming curfews. "Obviously, we had curfews. At 10 P.M. the computer had to be off. We fought about it for years. Other parents have told me their sons will go to bed and they'll wake up and hear him on the computer and it would be 2 A.M."

Referring to the research findings in Wilmette, where upper-middle-class boys were falling behind, Fisher said, "People do traditionally think boys do better in school and have no idea that boys are actually being lost in the bottom half of the class." Video games lead to a withdrawal from school life, including academics, said Fisher. Speaking as the psychologist she is, Fisher said parents and teachers don't realize the impact school withdrawal has on the boys. "To be behind in the academic world for the first twelve years of your life, that's not a benign process. It's not benign that you don't fit well into an environment and don't feel like you can thrive. That's not something that most kids recover from so easily."

The evidence so far seems like an airtight case for convicting video games and their digital coconspirators. But are video games really that bad for boys? Obsession? Rather than blame video games, educators and parents could draw lessons from boys' obsession with the games, argues Thomas Newkirk, an English professor from the University of New Hampshire and author of *Misreading Masculinity*.[7] If anyone would be justified in pointing a blaming finger at video games it would be Newkirk, an expert on lapses in boys' reading and writing abilities. But that's not how Newkirk sees it. Video games appeal to boys because they give them "flow," says Newkirk, something akin to the soothing, positive mental charge readers get from a great book. Only many boys aren't reading, which leave video games as a more likely source of flow. Playing video games, says Newkirk, "is hardly mindless visual stimulation. When I watched my nephews play video games . . . I was dazzled by the split-second decision making, the calculation, the shifting from mode to mode. When I tried it, I felt like a total bumbler, hopelessly overmatched. While schools promote strategic thinking and problem solving, I imagine that for adept players . . . the video game is a much richer cognitive experience."

Even the most certain of evils about video games, that violent games encourage children (boys) to become more aggressive, is under reconsideration. Two researchers from Massachusetts General Hospital's Center for Mental Health and Media drew on Justice Department research to write their book, *Grand Theft Childhood*.[8] The husband-and-wife team, who became interested in the subject after watching their own son become immersed in video games, arrived at this conclusion: "For most kids and most parents, the bottom-line results of our research can be summed up in a single word: relax."

That advice, *relax*, is not likely to assuage parents who can see their sons become more aggressive after watching violent cartoons or video games. And fresh evidence of addiction to video games continues to emerge. In April 2009, a study drawing on national survey data concluded that 8.5 percent of youths in the United States between 8 and 18 showed signs of video game addiction.[9] "Symptoms included spending increasing amounts of time and money on video games to feel the same level of excitement; irritability or restlessness when play is scaled back; escaping problems through play; skipping chores or homework to spend more time at the controller; lying about the length of playing time; and stealing games or money to play more."[10]

That's alarming, but for purposes of determining the cause of the gender gaps the key question is: Which comes first, the gaming obsession or the withdrawal from school? While Fisher at first blamed video games for the school withdrawal, additional reflection moved her to a conclusion that things didn't happen in quite that order. "Boys can sometimes think of school as a feminine enterprise. A lot of their school books were not things that riveted them." By contrast, video games, especially the blood-soaked, first-person-shooter, complex games requiring strategy, pull them right in. Fisher is no fan of video games, but she agrees the disengagement came first. "I think boys are finding their victories elsewhere."

Fisher has a point, even if it's not provable by numbers. For many boys, the problem with video games is less the entrapments of "World of Warcraft" than the force that drove the boys to pull away from school in the first place. Once that school disaffection takes place, there's one easy place to find competence and, yes, flow, and that's with video games. Parents and teachers see the video game obsession and automatically assume the games, rather than the disaffection, lie at the heart of the problem. I don't count myself as a fan of video games, either. I tend to lean toward parents who say they do inflict harm. But the case for blaming video games for the gender gaps is problematic.

IT'S A LACK OF MALE TEACHERS

One day sixth grade teacher Jeff Plane noticed a couple of cheap, colorful beach balls for sale and had a thought: Why not turn them into a cool teaching tool?[11] So he bought two and inked in a simple literary question in each color panel on the balls. Catch the ball and you have to answer the question where your left thumb ends up: What's the main idea of the book? What's the setting? How did the story end? On this day, I'm sitting in the back row of Plane's class watching as he grabs the ball and tosses it without warning to a boy at Alston Middle School just outside Charleston, South Carolina. Suddenly, all the boys in the class come alive. Not only do they want to get their hands on that ball, they don't appear to mind the trade-off of having to answer the question. Many of the boys in Plane's class call him coach; he doubles as a football coach. The books Plane assigns are often boy-friendly books involving sports and action themes. Plane keeps a close eye on his boys, knowing that in his class gender is a better predictor of academic success than race. Here, the black girls far outperform the black boys and often best the white boys as well. Just by looking around his room, Plane grasps what many education reformers resist admitting: Solving racial learning gaps starts with whittling down the gender learning gaps.

Perhaps Plane is the kind of teacher reflected in the research of Thomas Dee, a Swarthmore College professor who in the fall of 2006 released research showing that middle school students learn best from teachers of their own gender.[12] Considering that roughly 80 percent of the teachers in U.S. public schools are female, the highest percentage of females in forty years, Dee's research proved controversial. Based on a survey of nearly 25,000 eighth graders, Dee examined how students fared in three subjects—science, social studies, and English—based on the gender of their teachers. Girls did better with a female teacher; boys fared better with a male teacher. Part of the explanation may be how teachers view discipline issues, says Dee. "Regardless of the academic subject, boys are two to three times more likely than girls to be seen as disruptive, inattentive and unlikely to complete their homework," writes Dee, drawing from teacher surveys. "These results suggest that part of boys' relative propensity to be seen as disruptive in these grades is due to the gender interactions resulting from the preponderance of female teachers." Boys suffer most from the gender gap, says Dee, simply because most middle school teachers are female. In his sample, 83 percent of the eighth grade reading teachers were female. "My estimates suggest that, if half of the English teachers in sixth and seventh and eighth grades were male . . . the achievement gap in reading would fall by approximately a third by the end of middle school." If Dee is right, then the scarcity of male teachers in middle schools could be a significant player in the gender gaps.

Problem is, I'm skeptical that a surge in the number of male teachers would have that impact. My sense is that the impressive performance I witnessed in Jeff Plane's class says more about good teaching than about male teaching. What makes all this so confusing is that the time line tracking the decline in boys' performance in school roughly matches the time line of the decline in the number of male teachers. And when looking at black boys, the correlation seems especially powerful. Black boys, sociologists tell us, are more affected by fatherless families than black girls, which helps explain why black girls fare so much better in school. Given the dearth of black male teachers to make up for the lack of male role models at home, should anyone be surprised that so many black boys fail in school? Black male teachers continue to disappear, say school administrators. In Florida, they make up a mere 3.2 percent of the teaching population.[13] Within the predominantly African-American student body at Florida A & M University's College of Education, some students view teaching more as a transient form of public service, akin to serving in the Peace Corps, than as a life's work.

While I can't deny the power of the logic, I'm still not convinced that campaigns to dramatically boost the number of male teachers would turn around the gender gaps. The schools I visited that succeed with boys paid scant attention to the number of male teachers. Good teaching, combined with a determined "no excuses" attitude where teachers were determined not to let a single child fall behind, including the boys, proved to be the difference, not hiring more male teachers. Some of the most successful education innovators appear to lean on strategies other than boosting the number of male teachers. In the KIPP (Knowledge Is Power Program) school I profile later in the book that does a spectacular job educating inner-city boys, male teachers make up a small percentage of the staff.

The same holds true for the widely admired Teach for America program, which recruits graduates from elite colleges to teach in inner-city schools. "Our own data hasn't shown that men are more effective," says founder Wendy Kopp. Among Teach for America's 2008–2009 teacher corps, 70 percent are female. Kopp knows exactly what she's looking for in teachers, and it has little to do with gender. "I just came from interviewing someone who was applying for a marketing job here. She said she never personally wanted to teach, that she didn't have the patience for it. That's one of the things we fight. We're not looking for patience. We're looking for someone who is achievement-oriented, someone who is a real leader. They need to set goals and motivate kids to work toward those goals." At Teach for America, women are as likely as men to emerge as aggressive goal setters, said Kopp.

Kopp has a good point. While the fact that researchers have uncovered a slight advantage when students are taught by an instructor of the same gender is interesting, that doesn't seem to be the most important factor. And while the dearth of male role models, especially at the middle school level, is regrettable, that can't account for the fact that middle school is the time when gender gaps blossom. There's a far stronger force acting on boys at those ages.

I'm not suggesting that recruiting more male teachers would be a mistake. As Bryan Nelson of MenTeach, a Minneapolis-based group that tries to recruit more male teachers, once told me: Why would a boy think attending school was meaningful or important to him if there are no men there? Nelson has a point. There are good reasons to hire more male teachers. Expecting to solve the boy troubles with male teachers, however, should not be one of those reasons.

IT'S (ONLY) THE BLACK BOYS

In 2004 the Schott Foundation for Public Education handed Michael Holzman an education researcher's dream job: Find Ohio high schools to honor for succeeding with African-American males and tell the story of their success. Holzman, a veteran Ph.D. researcher who has overseen many of the foundation's reports on the plight of black males, spent months sifting through data from roughly six hundred Ohio high schools. Holzman's definition of success was relatively simple. Black males had to graduate at a rate of at least 70 percent and their test scores had to roughly match those of the other students. In the fall of 2005 the foundation selected three high schools to honor and sponsored a college scholarship at each school. Here's the story behind the story: The three schools honored were the only ones that met that criteria. "There weren't a lot. There weren't four high schools."

Then the Schott Foundation decided to take the search national. Once again, Holzman got the task, this time sifting through several thousand high schools. In January 2007, Schott honored three high schools, one in Ohio and two in New York. Here's the story behind the national search: Among schools that are majority black, Holzman found only two that met his criteria. Holzman's exhaustive search to find black males succeeding anywhere in school in this country nicely captures this problem. Optimistic statistics about black males are a rarity, which is why pushback writers, those who say the boy troubles are exaggerated, argue that the only boy problems are about race and poverty. Those making the argument that all efforts should focus on black boys have no shortage of data:

- Low high school graduation rates. Only about 48 percent of black males earn diplomas, compared to 59 percent of black females. Nationally, 70 percent of all students graduate from high school.[14]

- Low college attendance rates. Black women earn college degrees at twice the rate of black males.

- Low college graduation rates. More than two-thirds of black male students who enroll in college fail to graduate within six years.[15]

- Poor employment among dropouts. In 2000, 65 percent of black males in their twenties who dropped out of high school were unemployed. By 2004 that climbed to 72 percent. Black high school graduates barely fare better, with half unemployed in 2004.

- High incarceration rates. Twenty-one percent of black males who did not attend college were in jails or prisons in 2004.

> Among blacks who dropped out of school, 60 percent have
> spent time in prison by their mid-thirties.[16]

Some selective colleges have become so desperate to find motivated, academically qualified black males that they reach into middle schools to find
potential candidates worthy of mentoring through high school. California
State University chancellor Charles Reed conceived of "Super Sunday,"
where CSU campus presidents fanned out across the state to appeal to black
church congregations to send them students, especially males. At CSU's
twenty-three campuses, two of every three black students are female.[17]

There are no silver linings in the facts about young black males in
school. But does that make the boy troubles all about poor and minority
boys? The arguments making that case come from skeptics of the boy
troubles who argue that the gender problems are both exaggerated and
confined to poor and minority boys. Many doubters point to the monograph "The Truth About Boys and Girls," written by education analyst
Sara Mead when she worked at the think tank Education Sector.[18] Mead
contends that most boys are doing reasonably well. Writes Mead: "There's
no doubt that some groups of boys—particularly Hispanic and black boys
and boys from low-income homes—are in real trouble. But the predomi-
nant issues for them are race and class, not gender. Closing racial and
economic gaps would help poor and minority boys more than closing gender gaps, and focusing on gender gaps may distract attention from the
bigger problems facing these youngsters."

If arguing that race rather than gender is behind the gender gaps is
an attempt to keep the focus solely on reducing racial learning gaps, then
I'll concede that's a noble goal, at least on the surface. I've spent a fair
amount of my career writing about closing those racial learning gaps,
which are proving extraordinarily difficult to narrow. The question, however, is whether it's possible to close those gaps while ignoring the influence of gender. To answer that, let's look at the Chicago Public Schools, a
mostly African-American school district where some of the most exacting
school research in the country has been carried out by the University of

Chicago–based Consortium on Chicago School Research. Contrary to what Mead writes, the Chicago researchers conclude that gender is a significant factor. Veteran school researcher Melissa Roderick dubs this the "genderization of race." African-American boys and girls coming from the same neighborhood, the same families, and the same schools are turning out radically different, with the girls succeeding (by urban Chicago standards) and the boys faltering.

The argument that race and poverty, not gender, drives the boy troubles also ignores the spreading number of upper-middle-class high schools discovering large and unexpected gender gaps among their students. As described in Chapter 1, educators and parents alike at the Wilmette schools in the pricey neighborhoods just outside Northwestern University were shocked at the gender gaps uncovered in a unique investigation there.

The difficulties African-American boys are having in public schools are profound. They easily qualify for the overused "crisis" tag. But to say the problems are solely rooted in race and poverty ignores both the gender gaps among black students and the gaps found in upper-income suburban schools. Denying those realities only postpones interventions that could make a difference for boys.

IT'S A MEDICAL PROBLEM

The afflictions that disproportionately affect boys include autism and attention-deficit hyperactivity disorder (ADHD). Although estimates vary depending on the survey, it appears safe to say that boys are roughly four times as likely as girls to be diagnosed with these disorders. When looking for possible links between these disorders and the boy troubles, it makes sense to examine each separately.

Autism

In February 2007 the Centers for Disease Control and Prevention produced front-page stories around the county with the release of a study showing that far more children suffered from autism than previously believed—as many as one in every 150 children and one in 100 boys. States such as New Jersey, which are credited with high per-pupil spending and a sophisticated network for identifying autistic children, had the highest rate of autism and the steepest gender gaps. For every 1,000 boys in New Jersey, 16.8 suffered from autism, compared to 4 per 1,000 girls. Researchers dismissed any environmental causes for the high rates in New Jersey. Other states would discover similar rates if they looked closely. "We have a sensitive system and unfortunately we're picking a lot of cases up," said Dr. Walter Zahorodny, director of the New Jersey Autism Study, which was part of the survey. "If they had the ability to do it as accurately in other places, it might be as high everywhere else."[19]

The question of why so many boys are diagnosed with autism is addressed by the National Autistic Society, which sifts through the various theories.[20] Autism is a "spectrum" of disorders, ranging from mild to severe. It's possible that girls with mild forms of autism "may be better at masking their difficulties in order to fit in with their peers. . . . Boys with the same level of disorder are more likely to stand out." Other researchers posit that autism is an exaggeration of normal sex differences. The fact that boys tend to be less verbal than girls could explain why the language and communication problems displayed by autistic children is more obvious in boys.

Autism appears to arise from a combination of genetic and environmental triggers, either of which can explain why boys are more vulnerable. At birth, boys are more medically vulnerable than girls. On the genetic side, researchers are focusing on the X chromosome, which boys inherit only from their mothers but which girls inherit from both parents. Something in the father's X chromosome may to some extent protect girls from autism. In the end, the society concludes that research has yet to pinpoint the exact reason why so many more boys than girls suffer from autism. Regardless of the cause, the autism trend affecting boys appears to be moving on a separate track from the boy troubles, which involve medically healthy boys becoming disaffected with school.

ADHD

The number of boys lining up at school to take attention-focusing drugs such as Ritalin has been the focus of many headlines in recent years. While the National Institute of Mental Health estimates that between 3 and 5 percent of children suffer from ADHD, the diagnosis rate swings wildly from one school district to another. Too often the first reaction to an attention problem is "Let's medicate."

Kids in Catholic schools are less likely to be on medication, while just the opposite holds true for kids from military families. White boys are twice as likely to be diagnosed with ADHD as African-American boys, which leads to suspicions about academic expectations: When white boys underperform is there an assumption of a physical problem, whereas black boys are just expected to underperform? One study comparing two similar cities in Virginia discovered that fifth grade is the peak year for ADHD diagnoses, with as many as one in five white boys taking medication at school.[21] In one city, old-for-grade students were more likely to be on medications, whereas just the opposite was true for the other city, where nearly two out of three young-for-grade students were on medication. Two out of three? That astonished the investigators.

The ADHD treatment practices by parents and physicians can only be described as erratic. Educators pressing for medication are no better. One misconception shared by all three groups may be the assumption that children afflicted with deficit disorders are academically doomed. Just the opposite may be the case, an international team of researchers recently concluded in a study of one thousand children. Those displaying disruptive and antisocial behavior in kindergarten fared no worse academically in elementary school than their peers.

Neither attention-deficit afflictions nor the overprescribing of drugs such as Ritalin appear to be major factors in aggravating the gender gaps. Rather, they are troubling reminders that until the underlying problems are solved, misdiagnoses and prescription abuse are inevitable.

IT'S THAT HOMEWORK HELPS GIRLS, HURTS BOYS

Several years ago I visited High Point Central High School outside Greensboro, North Carolina, a school that serves so-called "average" students. While at the school I learned that the dreaded "nine-week list" had just been sent home to parents. That's the list that fingers any student receiving a D or F for the grading period. I asked the school staff to conduct a quick computer run: What was the ratio of boys to girls on that list? It didn't take long to spit out an answer: 412 boys and 303 girls. There's nothing extraordinary about that figure. Boys account for roughly 70 percent of the D's and F's handed out, say educators. And homework is one of the biggest reasons for the grade gap, we're told. Teachers always point out that boys are far less likely to complete homework than are girls. The homework theory probably makes sense to mothers of boys, who often find their son's homework buried deep in the backpack—completed, perhaps, but never turned in.

The most prominent of the blame-homework theorists is William Draves, the author of several education books. Draves argues that in many ways boys outperform girls in school. Homework problems—homework turned in late or totally disregarded—drag down their grades, says Draves. He and co-author Julie Coates created the smartboysbadgrades .com website to help parents with the homework dilemma. "A major reason why smart boys do not turn homework in on time is that boys are neurologically geared towards unsolved problems and challenges. That is, if they do not know it, they focus on it. If they already know it, it becomes 'boring' and is very hard to focus."[22]

In school, boys turn in homework late or show up late to school for the same reason, argues Draves. They're bored. So why, then, do they show up for a boring job on time? "There's a tangible outcome to work, and no tangible outcomes for schoolwork," say the authors. "There is a visible reward for turning work in on time, and no reward for turning schoolwork in on time." As a reason why many boys fail to turn in homework, that makes sense. My interviews with boys during school visits for this book reveal another reason: It's just not cool to be a grade grubber. If you show your guy friends you did your homework but don't bother turning it in and accept the lower grade, well, that wins you tough-guy points.

The most important step any school can take to level the gender gap is to stop punishing students who turn in their homework late, argue Coates and Draves.

Could the boy troubles really be explained by something as simple as homework? Eliminating the homework penalty *would* ease the growing grade gap between boys and girls. But I'm skeptical that homework problems lie at the core of the gender gaps. One reason is that girls have pulled ahead of boys not only in grades but in test scores as well, which have little to do with homework. That's what Paul Reville, then head of the Rennie Center for Education Research & Policy in Massachusetts (he later became superintendent of schools for Massachusetts) discovered when he examined the state's ten largest school districts.[23] After seeing the national data on gender gaps Reville decided to investigate where the boys and girls stood in Massachusetts. While he expected to find significant grade gaps, and did, what surprised him were the state test scores. "We found in virtually every category, grades four through ten, that girls had the edge in test scores, even in math, where historically boys have done better." Is that because the urban schools are poorer? No. What Reville found in Massachusetts is exactly what Superintendent Glenn "Max" McGee found in the wealthy Wilmette district outside Chicago: Girls are pulling ahead not only in grades but in test scores as well. Yes, girls do reap a considerable grade advantage for turning in their homework on time. And yes, the higher grades make them more competitive when applying to colleges. That makes homework a player in the gender gap, but not the key player.

IT'S THAT FEMINIZED CLASSROOMS TURN OFF BOYS

Among boy advocates, this is an article of faith. Here's how the theory plays out: The ever-rising percentages of female teachers (more than 90 percent of elementary teachers and three-fourths of all teachers) has reached a tipping point where the classroom culture has changed. Now only students willing to sit quietly in their seats, write neat letters, and complete all class assignments on time get rewarded. As for where that leaves fidgety, headstrong boys, well, you know how that story turns out.

The boy advocates have a point. Male teachers are more likely to tolerate behaviors that may be threatening to some female teachers, such as standing for periods of time or stretching out under the desk. Many parents of boys will attest that their young boys only marginally fit into today's highly structured classrooms. "The image of a schoolchild as someone sitting and reading has become the poster image for education, especially in the last fifty years," writes Michael Gurian in *The Minds of Boys*.[24] "This is not a bad image—but it is an incomplete match with the way the minds of many of our boys work." Boys, says Gurian, are blessed with a furious "boy energy" that warrants respect.

"Our homes and buildings are built by it. Our roads are laid down in its vision. Our rocket ships fly because of it. . . . Boys learn through impulsive trial and error, then become the men who, as lawyers or doctors or athletes or corporate managers, force innovation into the human theater."

Gurian and other boy advocates lay out exacting conditions for how boys learn best. Teachers who follow their guidance settle on a quick-moving teaching style with lots of breaks and movement. I have seen the boy-specific learning styles recommended by Gurian and others in action and they can be very effective. This is especially true with regard to reading programs geared to boys' interests. As a reporter, however, I have to add that I've seen gender-neutral approaches work just as well.

In the end, I don't view feminized classrooms as the source of the problem. Elementary schools have always been staffed with nearly all female teachers, including during the times when boys were doing far better in school. (I should mention that higher education consultant Tom Mortenson, the dean of the gender gap experts, disagrees with me on this one, maintaining that today's female teachers are schooled in a feminist dogma that leaves them resistant to the idea that boys need to be taught in different ways.)

IT'S THAT TOO MUCH TESTING HURTS BOYS

What boy wouldn't agree with the suggestion that he's slipping behind in school because teachers give him too many tests? It turns out this theory has proponents other than tenth grade boys who dislike tests. In fact, the highly regarded reading experts Michael Smith and Jeffrey Wilhelm cite No Child Left Behind, the test-heavy school federal reform law, to explain in part why they think boys are faltering in school.

"There is a feeling in this country that there's a crisis in education," said Smith. "What schools have done in response is to keep school the way it is, but deliver more of the same. More homework, more summer reading." And, of course, the extra testing that accompanies that. But that only backfires, says Smith. "Kids who are resistant (to education) now have more to resist. Boys who are falling behind in reading are told, 'Let's have a summer reading list' that dictates to them what they are supposed to do over the summer as well. So here's a kid who hated reading for ten months being told he has to read through the summer. I don't see how that helps anyone, especially since summer reading is assigned without providing any instruction to help kids understand and enjoy what's assigned."

Co-author Wilhelm agrees. "No Child Left Behind is the problem. . . . You get huge pressure from schools to meet AYP (adequate yearly progress . . . evidence that learning is taking place). Particularly in the (poorer) schools kids are being made to do more from the scripted (phonics) programs. . . . Those are totally unmotivating. They are missing all the magic of literacy." The use of phonics is only part of what's needed to turn boys into readers, said Wilhelm. "Kids who most need a rich literacy program, real reading, real assistance, are put into these programs where they are doing drill and kill stuff." Are Wilhelm and Smith right? Is the standards movement, which triggered a bevy of new tests tied to scripted reading programs, the reason boys are falling behind in school? Yes and no. The answer requires a bit of history.

The modern education reform movement started in 1989 after the nation's governors met in Charlottesville, Virginia, and walked away with an agreement that all students would benefit from a high school curriculum preparing them for college. As any college student knows, a college curriculum is heavily dependent on reading and writing skills. In the upper grades, principals responded to the Charlottesville challenge by doing their best to lure more students into the verbally difficult advanced placement courses. In that environment, more girls than boys will thrive.

But the real impact played out in the elementary school years. To prepare shaky readers for the verbal challenges in later grades, educators ushered phonics-heavy reading programs such as Open Court into the early grades. That was the right action to take. Thousands of boys have been steered into special education solely because they failed to get the kind of phonics training provided by programs such as Open Court. On the other hand, a boy who receives nothing more than a daily dollop of Open Court may get turned off to reading. And in some cases, even that's not enough.

I spent several months observing Jacob, an obviously bright boy in a Maryland fifth grade classroom where the teacher not only used Open Court but supplemented it with boy-friendly extra reading. Unfortunately, best efforts don't always produce results. Jacob learned to play the school literacy game—completing classroom reading and writing tasks—and yet continued to prove resistant to reading anything beyond what was required in school. Unless something dramatic happens with Jacob in the next couple of years, I have a hard time imagining him capable of handling college-level reading and writing.

The real damage from the standards movement appears to be in writing, the skill where boys have fallen fastest. In the Maryland schools I observed, students were forced to funnel any writing talents into highly formulaic short essays designed to match the Maryland writing test. When writing gets reduced to this kind of drill-and-kill exercise, the winners are students who are most classroom-compliant, most willing to do schoolwork for the sake of schoolwork, most able to form perfect letters, and most eager to please the teacher. That would not be your average fifth grade boy.

So the testing critics have a point. I have a hard time conceding that, given that while writing for the *USA Today* editorial page we championed the school accountability movement that requires testing. For too long too many students, especially poor and minority boys, were getting left behind. And yet, while I continue to support the need for test-dependent accountability, I can see real damage being done to boys whose budding interests in reading and writing are often crushed by unimaginative teaching and testing. So from my perspective, that makes testing a player in the gender gaps. Not the biggest player, but a player.

IT'S THE TOXIC CULTURE

You name it, from rapper 50 Cent to the video game "Grand Theft Auto," the answer to boys falling behind comes back the same: toxic culture. Boys, far more than girls, get sucked into the culture, especially African-American males. Harvard researcher Ron Ferguson once attempted to chart the impact rap music had on young black men.[25] In the early and mid-1980s, black boys made significant strides in closing the historic academic gaps with whites, said Ferguson, a contributor to the book *The Black-White Test Score Gap*.[26] "In a generation or two we could have just about wiped out the gap," said Ferguson at a Brookings Institution press conference in 1998.

But the progress stopped abruptly in 1988. In fact, racial learning gaps have not closed since that time. What happened? Two things happened in 1988 that could solve the mystery—crack cocaine and the explosion in popularity of rap music with its school-ain't-cool message. "Even kids not part of the street culture took that on as their identity," said Ferguson. "It could be an important part of why the gains stopped."

It doesn't take a Harvard researcher to tell you that the "acting white" phenomenon (doing well in school is a "white" trait to be shunned) had a huge impact on boys, including white boys, thousands of whom adopted the hip-sounding message of the rap musicians. Any teacher can tell you that even the most academically inclined white boys often try to disguise their achievements. In middle-class high schools, white boys get away with it because their well-off parents always manage to find a college for them to attend regardless of their slacker high school record. (While the news coverage always focuses on the highly selective colleges that are swamped with applications, hundreds of colleges are more than eager to recruit males with parents able to foot the tuition bills.)

So that's it? The hip-hop culture launched in the late 1980s first infected black males and then spread to white males as well? It's tempting to embrace the theory as the source of the boy troubles, but it's not really logical. As an explainer of the boy problems, the hip-hop theory runs aground when put into international perspective. The international benchmarks for judging gender gaps are set by the Organization for Economic Cooperation and Development, which finds widening gender gaps in most Western developed countries. Especially wide gender gaps are found in Greece, Iceland, Ireland, Italy, Portugal, and Spain, according to the surveys. Can the influence of 50 Cent explain trends in Iceland and Portugal? That would be a stretch. As gratifying as it might be to blame violent and misogynistic rap lyrics for the gender gaps, I'm forced to concede that 50 Cent can't be held accountable as the villain, at least not for that.

IT'S THE BOY CODE MORPHING INTO THE GUY CODE

The "boy code" arises from the work of clinical psychologist William Pollack, director of the Center for Men at McLean Hospital, a mental health hospital that is part of Harvard Medical School. "Over the last several years, I and other professionals who work with boys have become increasingly aware that even boys who seem OK on the surface are suffering silently inside—from confusion, a sense of isolation, and despair. They feel detached from their own selves, and often feel alienated from parents, siblings, and peers. Many boys feel a loneliness that may last throughout boyhood and continue into adult life."[27] That confusion and isolation, says Pollack, explains why boys make up more than two-thirds of special education classes, are ten times more likely than girls to be diagnosed with a serious emotional disorder, and lag behind girls in school.

The problems arise, according to this theory, when boys are pushed away from their mothers too soon. "Mother is expected to 'cut the apron strings' that tie the son to her and, indeed, that connect him to the entire family. As early as age five or six, many boys are pushed out of the family and expected to be independent—in school, at camp. . . . We give our boys in early adolescence a second shove—into new schools, sports competitions, jobs, dating, travel and more." Many boys aren't ready for that early break and "feel ashamed of their vulnerability." But whining or stalling is shunned by parents who feel boys must start to establish their independence.

As part of that early hardening, boys feel expected to live up to a harsh, unwritten boy code that commands them to be strong and independent and to suppress emotions, writes Pollack. "The code is a set of behaviors, rules of conduct, cultural shibboleths, and even a lexicon, that is inculcated into boys by our society." Boys' discomforts with the code account for the higher rates of violence, suicide, school failures, and other maladies, writes Pollack. "I believe that an overwhelming number of elementary school boys diagnosed with conduct disorders or with what is often called attention deficit disorder, or ADD, are misbehaving not because they have a biological imbalance or deficit but because they are seeking attention to replace the void left by their mothers and fathers."

When Pollack's boys leave childhood, they enter "Guyland," described in Michael Kimmel's 2008 book by that name.[28] As a boomer, I'm too old to know firsthand about Guyland, but I got a taste of it two years ago when my wife and I decided to move to the Courthouse/Clarendon neighborhood in northern Virginia to be within walking distance of a Metro. Within a few blocks of our house are corridors of restaurants and bars that by day draw a respectable and calm crowd from nearby offices. At midnight on a Friday and Saturday night, however, these joints become Guyland, a place where bands of buddies, many of them recent graduates of Virginia Tech or the University of Virginia, arrive to drink and party. The guys have decent jobs, but unlike twenty-somethings from previous generations, they're more invested in prolonging their adolescence than in settling down, getting married, having children, and working their way up the corporate ladder.

The promotion for his book describes the world Kimmel wrote about:

From coast to coast, from locker rooms to fraternity houses to sports bars, they're everywhere: packs of aimless young men in their late teens and twenties with seemingly nothing better to do than hang out and brag about how much they drank the previous night, their prowess playing the latest video games, or the random girls that they've "hooked up" with. Though the specifics of their individual situations may vary, these guys manage to fit into a single, common culture—Guyland—that supports a shocking set of behaviors which mask underlying feelings of uncertainty and self-doubt and, ultimately, keep many in a virtual netherworld between adolescence and adulthood, afraid and unable to take the necessary steps towards becoming responsible adult men.

Kimmel, a sociology professor and gender studies expert, is not alone in picking up on the significance of Guyland. Drawing on his years as a teacher, Joe Carmichiel wrote *Permanent Adolescence*, also published in 2008.[29] The promotion headline for Carmichiel's book reads: Is the Peter Pan complex ambushing today's boys? Carmichiel's book examines males a full socioeconomic notch below the white-collar men portrayed in Guyland. But the conclusions are similar. Excerpts from that book promotion read:

> Too many boys wish Neverland really existed so they can stay a child forever. It sounds like a lot of fun and games, with few adult responsibilities or chores. But what if a whole generation of males really didn't grow up? This is the escalating problem of a generation of lost boys who never really take on adult responsibilities, have trouble maintaining personal relationships and play games forever, or worse, violently act out. . . . As a teacher working with troubled boys as well as gang members, Carmichiel has discovered that males are getting stuck in a state of permanent adolescence. And how these male permanent adolescents are taking on key adult roles without having fully developed into adults. . . . Carmichiel examines the major reasons causing permanent adolescence: the disappearance of coming-of-age rituals; the effect of television on children's brain development; the lack of male role models; the normalization of violence; the inadequate teaching methods in schools. All these factors cause

boys to be contemptuous of adulthood, mistrust adults and, rather than seek mentorship or adult development, choose to remain permanent adolescents.

There is no doubt that Guyland exists, and Kimmel and Carmichiel do a great job describing it. But does Guyland explain boys falling behind in school and failing to earn college degrees? According to Kimmel, the overlap arises from the fear these guys have of appearing feminine. Remember the famous lines from the hit movie *The 40-Year-Old Virgin* (a true Guyland flick) where the two buddies sit side by side playing a death-match video game while swapping gay insults?

Every guy under the age of thirty recognizes the humor. From middle school through the frat house years, some guys define their manhood by declaring who they're not—as in, not gay. Sometimes it's seemingly harmless humor, as seen in the movie, but often it's ruthless taunting. The key tenet of Guyland, a palpable fear of being seen as feminine, explains the academic swoon boys have experienced in school, especially their reading skills, contends Kimmel. His theory greatly simplified: Reading is for girls.

So this is the answer for the gender gaps, Pollack's Real Boys melding into Kimmel's Guyland? Pollack's research is solid, built upon his clinical practice. Boys really do have those issues. When I visited California State University, Fullerton, to try to understand why women graduated at far higher rates than men, that macho element partly explained the go-it-alone attitude men had that got them into academic trouble.

I'm a reporter, not a sociologist or psychiatrist. For the sake of this book I'll assume that Pollack, Kimmel, and other writers who explore the oppressive boy code and guy code are on target. Much of it certainly rings true. But are these codes responsible for boys' poor reading abilities? That part leaves me uneasy. There is no reason to assume the neuroses Pollack describes were triggered only in recent years. If the boy code is a negative pull on boys it's been a negative pull for generations, including the years when boys fared far better in school. How can that explain the relatively recent swoon?

As for the guy code, that's a state Kimmel says boys enter in their mid-teens and depart in their mid- to late twenties. Boys and girls part ways in reading abilities early in elementary school, long before any reading-is-for-faggots teasing. I have no doubt that what Kimmel describes is a factor, but I remain skeptical that the guy code is a central player in the gender gaps. Kimmel is not the first to offer up the macho theory to explain the reading lapses. That theory holds that boys' unquestioning embrace of male-macho values not only views reading as a girls' activity but also stifles the introspection needed to develop verbal skills. Sounds good, but John Wayneism was around long before boys began their slide in school. Both Kimmel and Carmichiel wrote books about a phenomenon that's both true and important, but when it comes to the school gender gaps, I see the Guyland/Peter Pan complexes as more symptoms than causes.

* * *

Those are the major theories behind the gender gaps. (I left out the minor players such as boys are lagging because they're obsessed with cars. When, since the beginning of the car culture, has that not been the case?) While many theories have merit, none lie at the core of the problem. Perhaps a better way to get at the actual cause of the gender gaps is to examine schools that do well by boys. With a little reverse engineering it's possible to see both causes and solutions in their stories. I'll profile several of those schools in the next chapter.

CHAPTER 6

Solutions:
What Works for Boys?

AS A REPORTER, the only method I trust for determining what works for boys involves a lot of shoe leather. Here are three schools I located with the help of think tanks, school advocacy groups, and education foundations. The first, Frankford Elementary, is a traditional public school. The next is a single-sex New York City charter school. Charters are public schools with independent management. Finally, I profile a co-ed charter school in Washington, D.C., one of the highly regarded KIPP (Knowledge Is Power Program) schools. At the end of the chapter I will discuss what they have in common.

JUAN'S STORY

Frankford Elementary, Frankford, Delaware

The first thing you notice about fifth grader Juan is his hair, an elaborate concoction that starts with a generous dollop of hair wax. The thick black hairs at the back of his head get combed straight forward, while the short bangs in the front get raked upward at a 45-degree, ski jump sort of angle. It's a look. "Juan is going to be a ladies' man," teased one teacher there. Teasing always brings a big, easy smile from Juan. When Juan's parents, who speak no English, moved here from Mexico to find work they enrolled him as a third grader. As a reader of English, he tested in the preschool range.

In most schools in the United States, the fate of Juan would be predictable. His English-speaking abilities would steadily improve, mostly the result of cultural immersion. Poorly executed bilingual programs, however, would leave his English reading and writing skills at levels too low to hope for much beyond winning a high school diploma. At that point, he would join his father as a laborer or his mother in restaurant work. Being assigned to Frankford Elementary, however, is something akin to winning a school lottery. Here, that's not necessarily how boys such as Juan turn out. What makes the Frankford story so compelling is not just the ability to keep poor Latino and African-American students at grade level, or even higher, but that the boys leave this school with reading skills every bit as strong as the girls'.

Although Juan started here at the preschool level, halfway through his fifth grade year he's testing just slightly below grade level in reading skills. Given that he's in a school district determined not to lose those gains as the students move through the difficult middle school years, there's at least an even chance that Juan will have a shot at college. But there's something beyond academic competence the Frankford teachers unearthed in Juan. As it turned out, Juan has a great sense of humor that had been buried by language barriers. "Last year he was very quiet, barely spoke to anyone," said principal Duncan Smith, who once a week personally mentors Juan to improve his reading and writing skills. "Since I've started working with him I've seen his personality change. He's a very friendly boy with a great sense of humor. I like to tease him about his hair." Every so often when Smith sees Juan in the hallway he insists on placing a piece of paper atop his head, just to ensure the signature comb job is perfectly flat. That always brings out that big, easy smile.

The History Behind Frankford's Success

A beach-bound vacationer on the way to Delaware's Bethany Beach would have to get very lost to ever stumble across down-and-out Frankford Elementary. Although located only eight miles from Bethany's expensive beachfront homes, Frankford resembles a town lost in economic time. The twisting turns to the elementary schools take you by towering grain silos loaded with aromatic chicken feed. Ask Smith to name a single set of white-collar parents whose children attend his school and he puzzles over the question for at least a minute. He can't think of any. Latino students, who make up nearly 40 percent of the school, come from homes where their parents work in construction, landscaping, or chicken processing. Another third are African-American whose parents work either in the poultry plants or in the strip fast-food joints aimed at the transiting beach crowd. The balance of the school is white, most of whose parents are self-employed as contractors or house cleaners for the beach rentals at nearby Bethany Beach.

Tucked behind a menacingly tall metal security fence, the low-slung school building itself resembles a minimum-security juvenile facility. Only two blocks away is an open drug market. From time to time the children report their mother or father ended up in jail as a result of doing business there. Inside, the poorly lit building cries out for space and light. Most of the school lacks air conditioning. On rainy days it's best to keep the fan running in Smith's private bathroom here. Otherwise, the mold odors will pretty much lay you flat.

There's no way around concluding that Frankford Elementary resembles anything other than Delaware's sixth-top-performing school, beating out several far fresher-looking elementary schools that serve all-white professional families. Also impossible to believe is that this school could—if anyone bothered to inquire—serve as an example of how a school can turn out boys reading as well as girls. That wasn't the goal of the school reformers who triggered change here more than a decade ago. But it happened.

The story behind Frankford's success starts in 1995, when Sharon Brittingham arrived as principal. Brittingham, who had spent twenty-seven years as a middle school teacher and administrator in another Delaware district, could scarcely believe what she saw. The walls were dull, gunmetal gray; the carpet was seventeen years old. Drive-by shootings, an outgrowth of a nearby open drug market, were an occupational hazard. And then there was the issue of the stolen school bus. Beneath the surface, however, things were even grimmer. At that time, the school was half black, half white. Not only were nine of every ten African-American boys placed in special education, but the special education students were kept in a separate wing. They didn't even share lunch or recess with the other kids. Worse, the staff there thought that was the proper way to do business. "We had one little white girl qualify as special ed but the teacher told me, 'You can't put her in there with all those black boys.'" Most teachers there, said Brittingham, assumed the low test scores merely reflected the poor and minority population. The phrase was: "You can't make chicken salad out of chicken shit."

Brittingham devoted her first year at Frankford to listening and learning. Except for the special education apartheid. "I still remember the class pictures they used to take. The kids would gather with the teacher for a photo, and the top of the photo would say: Special Education." The Indian River district, along with several other Delaware districts, was under investigation by the federal Education Department's Office of Civil Rights for how special education students were handled, especially minorities. The civil rights investigation gave Brittingham the clout to act fast. The first year she mixed the special education classes in for recess and lunch; in the following years she mainstreamed nearly all the special education students.

The academic shortcomings at Frankford would take longer to sort out. Brittingham recalls going to district meetings where school test scores were posted. Frankford was always at the bottom. "Other principals would make comments like, 'That's pretty good for the kinds of kids you're dealing with.' I found that offensive." Being at the bottom also offended Brittingham's competitive nature. "I'm a former coach, basketball and field hockey. I once took over a hockey team that hadn't scored a single goal in five years. Eventually, we went on to become undefeated for several years." The fact that Brittingham had never played field hockey (or basketball) was seen by her as an advantage. "I really had to break down the sport and figure out, OK, what does it take to score goals?"

Brittingham, who had never worked in an elementary school, took the same approach at Frankford. Each student got his or her own individual learning plan, something other schools do only for their special education students. Brittingham rearranged the bus schedules so that children with the greatest academic needs got off first, went directly to the cafeteria for a quick breakfast, and then reported to a specific teacher to work on specific skills. That added up to an extra thirty minutes of instruction every day. Soon, the same was happening with after-school programs.

To shake things up even further at Frankford, Brittingham teamed up with a veteran reading expert at Frankford. "She and I are both very competitive people. If Frankford had a 'commendable' rating we'd ask, 'Why not a superior rating?' When other schools won the blue-ribbon award we thought, 'Why not us?'" In 2004 Frankford won a federal blue-ribbon award. Pulling that off meant tapping every grant possible to win extra curriculum support and the district's first full-day kindergarten. To boost reading scores, Brittingham made sure teachers had access to seven different methods for teaching reading. "We found there was no one reading method that worked with all children. If a child wasn't learning by phonics we would try something else." But no child disappeared in the system—they were all tracked by their individual plans.

At first, not all teachers were happy about the dramatic changes. "Sharon's philosophy was: 'We're here for the kids. You either change and make changes or go work somewhere else.'" Most teachers stayed and embraced the changes. Only three teachers who couldn't cope with the changes had to be forced out.

Taking Mentoring to a New Level

Nothing symbolizes the aggressive reforms at Frankford better than the mentoring program. When first designing the program, Brittingham recalls being told, "No tutors will want to come to Frankford." But just the opposite happened. "What we found was that everyone wanted to come to Frankford. They felt needed and it wasn't loosey goosey like the other schools. These people wanted to make a difference, and we were very structured."

Behind the success was Brittingham's decision to choose one of a handful of meaty programs that turn mentoring into a science. Frankford uses the HOSTS (Help One Student To Succeed) program, which breaks the mentor's job into short tasks, each carefully laid out in the HOSTS student folder that gets updated by the school staffer assigned to the mentoring program.[1] This checklist approach to tutoring allows modestly trained volunteers who may know little about the big picture of phonics instruction to carry out the small-bore tasks of phonics instruction like an expert.

A mentoring program that started out in 1999 with five mentors now has 160. At busy times of the day the mentors end up spread out in three classrooms. Roughly 120 students at Frankford see mentors, usually about three times a week for half-hour sessions. That's more than a fifth of the school population. To put this into perspective, most schools don't have mentoring programs that go beyond simple "role model" visits—bring a lunch, chat up a student, then leave. I did that at a local elementary school for a boy very much like Juan and considered it a waste of everyone's time—I wanted to be part of that boy's instruction, not his lunch adviser. The few schools that do have intelligent mentoring programs such as HOSTS or Book Buddies might have five or six mentors who show up once a week to mentor just one child. That makes Frankford mentoring on steroids. And it works. Not only do the students benefit from the literacy boosts, but the success of the school becomes a community success—all those state and national awards listed at the bottom of Frankford's Web page become community awards. Everyone earned them, not just the kids and the teachers, but also retirees who live at Bethany Beach but would never miss a mentoring date at this dowdy little school.

Several of the volunteer mentors come from the school staff. On Wednesday, Juan gets tutored by principal Duncan Smith. Among the other volunteer mentors at Frankford are the assistant principal and seven teachers, many of whom give up their daily planning period to mentor. Students here get assigned mentors on the basis of need. Juan, for example, received daily mentoring his first two years. Only now, in fifth grade, has he been cut back to three times a week. One of his mentors has been with him for all three years.

One mentor I met at Frankford on the April day I visited was a former probation officer for the District of Columbia. When he and his wife, who had worked as a nurse, retired to the shore they both signed up for mentoring through nearby St. Ann's Catholic Parish. "I try to create the kind of atmosphere where I can truly say, 'You're doing OK. I really like the way you write.' I find something legitimate to compliment them. I don't want to b.s. them. They're quicker at that than I am."

I visited Frankford in the fall and spring of the 2006–2007 school year. Since then, the overall success rate for the school has held up (with a different, but equally strong tutoring program), although in the 2008 tests girls moved slightly ahead of boys. The gaps were especially wide in writing, which is the case in nearly every school. But overall, the gender gaps have flattened, especially in reading, where at times the boys pull ahead of the girls, which is remarkable. In 2008, 100 percent of the fifth grade boys and 97 percent of the girls passed the state reading test. After fifth grade, the students head to middle school, which means the boys are well prepared for the upcoming literacy challenges.

THE SINGLE-SEX OPTIONS

Excellence Boys Charter School of Bedford-Stuyvesant
What seven-year-old boy wouldn't list fitness as his favorite school subject? Daniel, a second grader at this all-boys school I will follow through the day, is no exception. Not only does he have the chance to play football and soccer on the school's Astroturf rooftop field, but there's a spacious,

high-ceiling gym where in the winter months he can play tag and battle ball.[2] Yes, you heard that correctly, battle ball. At a time when some public elementary schools are banning tag (too aggressive), this charter school in one of New York's most famous high-poverty neighborhoods not only makes tag part of the official fitness program but battle ball as well, a game where boys from competing teams rush to the middle of the gym floor to push against a huge, weighted ball. First team to push it over a line on the gym floor wins.

In most schools the moment of victory would be celebrated with brash victory dances and trash talk. But that's not the way it works here at Excellence Boys Charter School, which is part of the Uncommon Schools network, a nonprofit that starts and manages high-performing charter schools that prepare low-income students to graduate from college. Here, the competing boys, all dressed in white shirts and ties, stop, look one another in the eye, shake hands, and say, "Good game." When the losers return to their sidelines they don't hear jeers but rather, "That's OK, better luck next time."

"We believe that competition can be an effective motivator for boys," said Jabali Sawicki, the founding principal of this charter school that in 2007 was in its third year of operation. "At the same time, students have to be taught how to compete with one another. It should be a motivation for trying to be your best, a motivation for trying to achieve. That's how we root this competition. The moment after the competition we talk about family and community, and how we're a team."

Competition is also encouraged in the classroom, but only as a self-motivator. "In math, teachers time them on exercises such as multiplication tables. They compete against themselves," said Sawicki. "Each week in school assembly we give out a spirit stick, a colorful stick that honors the students of the week. To win that, students compete in the classroom to show signs of respect and to help one another. It's something they treasure and work hard for."

The fifty minutes of exercise the boys here receive is called fitness, not recess. Every minute is overseen by a fitness teacher. "We decided not to have recess here," said Sawicki. "When you go to many traditional district schools recess is the time when boys tend to get into fights. And after recess the teachers have to spend forty minutes cleaning up what happened during recess."

The Origins of Excellence

After graduating from Oberlin College in 2001 with degrees in biology and philosophy, Sawicki took a job in Boston teaching science at Roxbury Preparatory Charter School, a school drawing students from one of Boston's poorest neighborhoods.

"Roxbury Prep is the highest performing urban school in Massachusetts," said Sawicki, "and yet I was struck by the discrepancies between boys and girls, especially the lack of success with some of the African-American boys. Here was this amazing school with amazing teachers and results, but something was awry with some of the boys." Sawicki tried to do what he could as a teacher, starting a science club for boys, coaching sports teams, and organizing a group of fathers and sons to meet for team-building exercises. But it never seemed enough.

Parallel to what Sawicki was doing in Boston, New York hedge fund mogul Paul Tudor Jones was looking for a way to continue the spirit of the "I Have a Dream Foundation," a program started in the 1980s to offer college scholarships to high-poverty elementary school students as an academic motivator. Eventually, Jones and other heavy-hitting benefactors created a new public charity, the Robin Hood Foundation, and a new strategy of reaching students early in life, especially boys, with the kind of high-quality schools lacking in the original I Have a Dream program.

"They decided to start an elementary school so you're not trying to cram into four years of high school what should be a thirteen-year job," said Sawicki. And when the benefactors pulled together charter school experts to look for an education leader with the vision to pull that off, the name pushed to the top was Jabali Sawicki.

To launch the first class of Excellence in 2004, Sawicki pulled the best of what he could glean from schools such as KIPP, Roxbury, the North Star Academy Charter School in Newark, and the Marva Collins Preparatory School, now located in Milwaukee. But there was major tweaking needed, in part because most of the successful urban charter schools were middle schools, not elementary schools, and they were co-ed, not all boys. From the other charters, Sawicki borrowed the longer school day and school year, 190 days a year from 7:30 A.M. to 4 P.M. That leaves time not only for fifty minutes of fitness but also daily art and music classes.

Most important, the longer days leave time to target what Sawicki concluded was the fundamental weakness of boys: poor literacy. Here at Excellence, boys receive two and a half hours of literacy instruction every day. Second graders such as Daniel experience multiple reading programs, ranging from highly scripted phonics programs to poetry. "With boys we have created a culture where reading is cool. We have a beautiful library stocked with amazing books. We've identified books that are especially appealing to boys. In contrast to most schools, when you ask boys here what their favorite place is, they'll say, 'The library.' "

How This Plays Out for Daniel

Try to imagine twenty second-grade boys sitting on the carpeted floor trying to come up with attributes common to a collection of poems they just read. Not too interested, you'd imagine. But not in Daniel's class, run by twenty-seven-year-old Meghan, who is calling on a plentiful showing of seven-year-olds raising their hands, some with impressive answers: Poems can sound like rap; poems can teach you facts; poems can be funny; poems can have words that "what's that big word you taught us"? (Onomatopoeia).

Now comes the big moment in the lesson. "This is an exciting day," said Meghan. "This is the day you get your own writer's notebooks." There's a low murmur of anticipation as she reaches behind her and drags out a big cardboard box full of thick notebooks, each with fancy hard covers.

As the teacher shows the boys her own writer's notebook, festively decorated with photos of her family and fiancé, the boys press forward and push a bit to get the best view. Voices pop up from the crowd. That's it! She slaps down the notebook, pushes away the box, and dispatches all twenty boys back to their desks.

In a voice that merged hurt and disappointment, the teacher lectured them. "Today was going to be a special day. I realize you were excited about getting the writer's notebooks but it was not fine to shout out. I love that you were so excited, but I don't love that you become so excited you forget how to behave as scholars." (The term "scholars" is used throughout the school to refer to the students.) Once the class settled, she turned to Daniel to ask why writer's notebooks were like seeds. Answers Daniel, "It's like a seed because first it doesn't have anything, then you add some writing. Its roots grow and then the whole thing grows." Not bad for a seven-year-old boy.

Later, over lunch, the teacher explained her "warm-strict" approach to teaching boys that prompted her to send all the boys back to their desks. She recalled her first day of urban education, teaching a fourth grade co-ed class at a public elementary school in Bedford-Stuyvesant. One boy threw something at her and when she started to discipline him another boy in the room coughed. Instantly, the first boy said to her, "He's allergic to white people." Recalls the teacher: "I shot back, 'Well, he's going to have to get over his allergy, because I'm here for you.'"

That's what she discovered about the boys. If you can prove you care about them, really care about them, they respond, and although boys get into more trouble than girls, that's only because girls are catty to one another, not to the teachers. "Boys still have that loving and nurturing side and society overlooks that. But boys need that, if you give them love, warm-strict love, they respond."

Daniel's Family

Native Trinidadians, Daniel's parents moved to the United States in 1995. They lived in a third-floor apartment, supported by Daniel's father, who works as a custodian at a New York public school. Before her second son, Simeon, was born, Daniel's mother worked at the Bowery Mission. When Daniel was in day care someone dropped off a flyer about Excellence Charter School. Later, his mother attended a talk Sawicki gave about his new school. "He gave a good speech about how disciplined it would be at the school and how they would have a strict dress code. That went along with what I had in mind for Daniel. And then when he talked about the curriculum he blew me out of the water."

To date, the parents are happy about the academics. Reading, the mother agrees, is not her son's favorite subject. But she stays on top of it, taking him to the library every other week for fresh books and making sure he reads every night. In true boy fashion, Daniel's favorite reading is nonfiction—a picture dictionary he keeps by his bed. "I pick out new words by the pictures that look interesting. I'll read six to seven new words a night." But for fun he'll also dip into fiction. "I like my Clifford books. My favorite is *Clifford Gets a Job*.[3] Clifford is a big red dog who was a little dog but got big by eating too many treats." While reading may not be Daniel's subject, he has turned the corner. Boys who never start reading for fun rarely succeed in later grades.

The mother is just as happy about the lessons of manhood and sportsmanship her son has picked up at Excellence. "He was not always good at sportsmanship. He would laugh if someone fell down or missed a shot. Sometimes he would cry if he lost. But now he's learning sportsmanship."

Results?

To build its school population, Excellence is adding a grade a year up to eighth grade. The school takes in seventy-five students per year in kindergarten. In its first three years, Excellence has averaged between two and three applications for every available spot. Students are offered positions through a lottery system.

The best barometer of success is Excellence's third grade class, the students who have been in the school for three full years. "When this class arrived, 37 percent were reading at or above grade level on the Terra-Nova," said Sawicki, referring to a national test that gauges where students rank nationally. The last time we tested our third graders 77 percent were reading at grade level." Math scores have gone up more sharply. Third graders started at 37 percent, but now 87 percent score at grade level.

"You wouldn't expect to find those gains in the vast majority of traditional urban public schools," said Sawicki. "They're about what you'd expect for a high-performing private school, making gains of about 10 to 20 percent a year. Our goal is to have all third graders reading at grade level by the end of the school year."

A final update: On the 2007–2008 report cards for New York City public schools, Excellence received an A and perfect score of 100, making it the top-ranked public elementary school in New York City.

In 2008 Daniel won the neighborhood (Bedford-Stuyvesant) spelling bee, beating out about forty students in his grade level. The top three finalists for his age group were all boys from Excellence. Daniel remains at the top of his class. Excellence plans to open an all-girls school in September 2009.

A CO-ED "NO EXCUSES" CHARTER

KIPP DC: KEY Academy, Washington, D.C.

Seventh grader Davon probably doesn't realize that his fate, and not a very promising one, was sealed until one fall day in 2003 when he walked into his third grade classroom and met his new teacher, Casey Fullerton, who was nervously facing her first-ever class of students. On that day, Fullerton was launching her two-year commitment with Teach for America, which trains recent graduates of top colleges to take on teaching assignments (and succeed) in the nation's toughest schools.

Fullerton grew up in tony Newport, Rhode Island, and graduated from Boston College. At five foot nine, with blondish hair, blue eyes, a never-ending smile, and the gait of a basketball player (which she is), Fullerton was destined to make a classroom impression. She had asked for a challenging school in the District of Columbia. "I thought if I'm going to be in the inner-city with a struggling school I might as well go to the one that's struggling the most."

She got her wish. Simon Elementary, Davon's neighborhood school, easily qualifies for that distinction. Davon lives in Southeast Washington, a racially isolated neighborhood of African Americans that middle-class white folks from Maryland, Virginia, and the better-off sections of Washington, D.C., have never seen, nor will ever see, in their lifetime. The grim crime headlines in *The Washington Post* are all they need to know about Southeast Washington.

If Davon had stayed on his current track that day, and managed to make it through middle school unscathed, he would have ended up at his neighborhood high school, Ballou, which was described in this manner in a 2006 *Washington Post* profile:

> Ballou is a sprawling circa-1960 school that sits on a hill on a quiet street in Congress Heights, across from a vacant lot where old tires, a mattress and a lamp have been dumped. The school has a large grassy campus with tall shade trees, but no one can use it because it is behind fences.
>
> Instead, the morning collection point for students is at the blue entry doors, where they line up and move single file through a metal detector and into a school that reflects much of the data reported across the country depicting how black males are at the bottom of

most academic measurements and experience the worst sociological outcomes. . . . Only about 9 percent of last year's 10th-graders were proficient in math—and 3 percent in reading.

Davon had all the early markings of yet another Ballou failure statistic. "He came in on his first day and couldn't fill out a sheet with his name and a list of his favorite things," recalls Fullerton. "He was unable to function, unable to read and write. It wasn't because he was a slow learner. He literally had gaps. He had not been instructed properly."

The first task was boosting Davon's confidence, getting him comfortable with coming to school. After that corner was turned, Fullerton was able to separate Davon and the other nonreaders into a separate reading group. In those groups, heavy doses of phonics instruction gave Davon the initial tools he needed to begin decoding language, a skill that should have been passed along far earlier in his schooling.

Davon stayed with Fullerton through fourth grade. "By fourth grade he was giving me 150 percent effort." But at the end of fourth grade, Fullerton concluded that Davon's modest gains would fade unless he found a way out of D.C. schools. The best option, Fullerton decided, was to convince Davon, along with five other struggling students she met at Simon, to transfer to Washington's KEY Academy.

Anyone visiting the KIPP (Knowledge Is Power Program) schools in Washington, or any of the other eighty-two KIPP schools spread over nineteen states and the District, will see classrooms run like no other classrooms in America. The KEY Academy, located in an unglamorous part of the District of Columbia just one Metro stop from the U.S. Capitol, takes kids from the district's low-performing elementary schools and in just four years puts them on a track to not only win acceptance to a college, but graduate from college. That, by itself, is enough to win KIPP the praise it deserves.

But there's another thing KIPP does that goes unnoticed, even by KIPP teachers. During my first visit to the KEY Academy, I paused in the hallway to study a posting of test scores. What I saw amazed me: In literacy skills, the seventh grade boys at KEY Academy scored even with the girls, maybe even a little ahead. When I asked the KIPP leaders in Houston if that happened in other KIPP schools, they took the time to run the numbers. After studying the data from several middle schools, they concluded it was no quirk. Boys arrive at KIPP schools in fifth grade reading roughly two years behind the girls, but by the end of seventh grade the boys, on average, read as well as the girls.

The folks at KIPP's Houston headquarters didn't seem particularly excited by the finding. Rescuing kids from awful urban schools is their mission, not leveling gender gaps. But I was intrigued, and here's why: KIPP succeeds with boys using methods that shred every bit of conventional wisdom about what works with boys. Those who assume that minority teachers serve as the best role models for minority students will find an all-black student body and nearly all-white faculty, at least at Davon's school. And while recent research shows that male teachers do better with boys, the KIPP faculty here is nearly all female.

Advocates for smaller class sizes, especially for inner-city children, will find class sizes no different from any traditional public school. Most interesting, the "brain-based" teaching theories about boys—they need to walk around a lot, experience hands-on learning, etc.—are not in evidence at KIPP, which enforces some of the toughest sit-at-your-desk, turn-in-your-homework policies you'll see anywhere short of military academies.

What KIPP does works, and it works with boys as well as girls. Anyone who has studied school reform turnarounds knows that KIPP is doing something that rarely happens, especially among middle school boys seemingly locked into the failures already handed them from the elementary school years. Had Davon continued on his former trajectory, I can imagine the conversation as his teachers recommended him for special education: Must be a hardwire problem in the brain, they tell the parents and principals. How else to explain a boy who can't read anywhere near grade level?

But Davon escaped that fate, in part from Fullerton's persistence and in part from the persistence of Susan Schaeffler, the founding principal of the KIPP schools in Washington, who is always looking out for talented Teach for America teachers rotating off their two-year commitments. Schaeffler lured Fullerton from Simon, so when Davon entered KIPP as a fifth grader, Fullerton took a job teaching sixth grade at KIPP. The following year Davon was in her class.

When Davon arrived at KIPP he tested in the fourteenth percentile on the nationally normed Stanford 10 achievement. By the end of sixth grade, he jumped to the forty-sixth percentile. To get an idea of how KIPP works I spent an entire day following Davon, now a seventh grader, from class to class.

Sept. 1, 2006

9:15 A.M.: Already, Davon has been in school since 7:45 A.M., the beginning of a day that often lasts until well after 5 P.M. Added to those long hours is mandatory summer school, which reduces summer vacation (the time when many students like Davon forget the lessons from the previous school year) to a single month.

Every homeroom at this KIPP school is named after the teacher's alma mater. Davon starts his day with his reading teacher Brenda, a recent graduate of the University of Oregon (hence, the name "Oregon" for Davon and his fellow classmates). For Davon's seventh graders, the homerooms are Boston College, Washington University, Wisconsin, Oregon, Bates, Citadel, Kansas, Loyola, and Northwestern. Every KIPP class is named after the year they will graduate from college.

"Okay, you have five minutes to pick out a book," Brenda tells half the class. "And remember the three-finger rule. If you come across more than three words on one page you don't know then find a different book."

Brenda tells half the class to leave their seats to find the books. The other half are to read at their desks. In nearly any

other school this would be an invitation for half the room to nois-
ily push back desks, scrape chairs, and wander around the classroom while the seated half caught up on the daily gossip. Here,
half the class really does read while the other half quietly sifts
through new book choices.

9:37: Another class changing classrooms silently passes by single
file in the hallway. No one in Davon's class even looks up.

9:40: Davon's class moves to science, where Kristen stands outside her room greeting each student: "Good morning, Oregon."
Whenever a student fails to make eye contact and respond with
"Good morning," the line stops until eyes meet and greetings are
exchanged.

 Davon, who is shorter than nearly every boy his age at KIPP,
dresses in khaki shorts, a black polo shirt, a small gold chain, and
New Balance running shoes. As always, there's a smile on his face.
He never fails the eye-contact test with Kristen.

9:43: Kristen learns from each student whether homework has
been completed. Undone homework is never excused, and it has
consequences that can lead to parents getting phone calls or,
worse, having the entire Oregon team docked points (student
groups here compete for rewards).

 Kristen fires up Oregon's team spirit with the lure of a science
field trip on a boat—if Oregon can outdo the other homerooms
on the myriad good-student measures KIPP uses. "You get to
catch snails and fish and everyone gets to drive the boat."

9:50: Voices rise and Kristen launches a short countdown. "Three,
two, one . . ." Complete silence. All these class-management de-
vices are drilled into "KIPPsters" in the first days of school orien-
tation.

9:55: Davon and his science partner are busy figuring out ways
to measure and describe the odd objects handed the team. Davon

hangs his rubber jellyfish from the desk, simplifying the measurement chore.

10:04: Davon raises his hand to answer a sophisticated question about scientific classifications. Boys in this class regularly raise hands to answer questions. None appear to fear looking too smart in front of the classmates.

10:16: Kristen tightens the full-length hooded sweatshirt she wears in the middle of summer. KIPP classrooms are kept at sixty-eight degrees, all the better to keep young minds focused.

Her classroom walls are filled with posters more about reading than about science. The parts of speech make up one large poster: article, noun, adjective, and so on. Another poster exhorts writing skills: "What are NO EXCUSE WRITING rules?"

10:43: Kristen explains the sixteen-point homework grading rules. This may be science class but writing skills make up twelve of the sixteen points, a reminder that at KIPP, regardless of the subject being taught, literacy skills remain at the forefront.

11:00: Lunch. All of Davon's teachers are in the cafeteria, often sitting down with students to discuss homework issues. Davon gets a visit from his math teacher to check on some homework.

Kristen lines up her seventh grade "leadership team"—all boys—to rehearse a surprise chant the seventh graders will unveil as they march into Friday's end-of-day assembly. "We're going to make an entrance like no others. . . . We want to be the grade everyone looks up to."

With an elaborate beat kept with clapping, the chest-pounding the seventh graders master:

Ready to go to college
To get some knowledge
To prepare to succeed
With everything I need
Go KIPPsters!

11:25: Lunch ends. Davon hasn't had time to touch his barbecue sandwich and only ate a few baked beans.

11:30: Spanish class with Melissa. Voices rise and the "Three, two one . . ." again works flawlessly. I am surrounded by kids wearing T-shirts that say "Assign yourself" or "No Excuse. No Shortcuts." A little intimidating. I catch myself worrying about whether I'm sitting up straight enough and exuding the right attitude.

11:35: Melissa has the front-row students demonstrate the proper technique for passing worksheets from row to row. After the demonstration, the entire class passes papers along neatly and quietly. No detail too small for special attention here.

11:44: Students writhing in their seats demonstrating the Spanish words for kicking a soccer ball and throwing a football. Nothing gets out of control, however. What might seem like oppressive discipline actually allows for more freedom among the students.

12:20: Math teacher Gillian greets Davon and the other students. "Good afternoon, Oregon!" One poster on the wall reads "Have you done your best?" Another poster states that scoring below 70% in this class is not acceptable. "To be successful in this class you should be getting 83% or better." Written at the top of one girl's worksheet: "Get to college or die trying."

And so the day continues, with every second of every minute micromanaged. It's exhausting. Not surprisingly, all the teachers appear to be in their twenties.

RETURN VISIT, MARCH 2007

Davon has a new reading teacher, Emily, after Brenda left for personal reasons. Emily, a recent graduate of the University of Pennsylvania, seems to know everything about Davon, especially his ongoing struggles with reading. Davon was one of a dozen or so seventh graders selected to get a booster course in phonics.

At first the group appeared embarrassed about being selected as slow readers. "But we all sat on the rug and talked about it. I told them about the high school class I once taught with three football players who couldn't read. Once they recognized they had the same struggle and didn't have to be embarrassed about it, they were really cute. Davon really took to it. Now, with his sounding out all the words, his reading skills are skyrocketing."

That's Davon's trademark. He may be the shortest seventh grade boy at KIPP and certainly not the strongest reader, but he has one of the sunniest dispositions.

"Outside of class, in flag football, he is a ball to watch," said Brian, his writing teacher and football coach. "We are currently [October] playing in a league that includes high school teams. He is easily the smallest player at the game at all times. Last week he was completely unafraid to enter the game to cover an opponent that was literally three times the size of him. After getting beat on the first two plays he came over to me and said, 'I want to play but I understand if someone else needs to go in.' That moment of maturity didn't last, as he began pestering me to get back in three plays later."

On this day Davon's reading class was studying *The Greatest*,[4] a biography of Muhammad Ali, a book Emily says she chose in part to reach more of the boys in her class. Emily said she noticed the boys weren't writing in their journals as much as the girls, and the boys doing the least amount of writing were the weakest readers.

"I come from a family of seven and have two brothers, so I went home and got all their books and brought them back here to get the boys more interested in reading. I didn't care what they were reading, *Sports Illustrated*, anything, just so they take to it and started reading other stuff.

The Ali biography proved to be a perfect choice. Davon loved it so much he earned the extra credit points required to take a personal copy home."

Says Davon, "It's one of the older copies of the book, but you get to take it home and write notes in it. I keep it in a drawer in my room." Davon estimates he has nearly two dozen books in his bedroom that he pulls out every so often to read. "I like action books, mysteries, solving crimes."

Davon agrees his reading skills are picking up in part because of the infusion of phonics. "I wasn't doing a good job before because I didn't know how to say a lot of the words. But now I'm doing a good job in reading."

KIPP's job with Davon is far from over. Recently, his grades dropped a bit, from a B-plus average to a C-plus average—enough to disqualify him from playing baseball and football for the KIPP team. Davon was set to get extra tutoring help, including an hour-a-day session with science teacher Kristen.

Will Davon leave KIPP as potential college material?

"Davon is the classic kind of kid who came to us with low skills and has been getting remediation since he's been here, and he's still receiving it," said principal Sarah Hayes, a tall blonde who looks as young as her barely-out-of-college teaching staff. With KIPP just a few blocks from the U.S. Capitol, she runs what may be KIPP's highest-profile school, drawing visitors who range from national policy experts to secretaries of education.

The KIPP system, a marvel to watch, works for boys and girls for the same reasons, said Hayes.

"Our whole curriculum and design is about catching kids up in fifth and sixth grades. We spend a lot of time focusing on the basics. With math, we start with single-digit addition on the first day of fifth grade and then work up to pre-algebra in sixth grade. We've designed our curriculum around the fact that we know kids are going to come in low. The fifth and sixth graders get three and a half hours a day of language arts."

KIPP's trademark "positive peer pressure" system is one reason KIPP schools reach boys who fail at other public schools, said Hayes. "The peer influence is so great at this age. It influences how they dress, whether they show up at school. We try to provide similar peer pressure but in the opposite direction. We try to do group incentives, like we do homeroom points, given to everyone who's there on time, in uniform, has their homework. So there's peer pressure to get to school on time and turn in your homework."

KIPP's seventh graders, for example, are competing to see which homeroom has the fewest students "on the bench" (a disciplinary move for students who falter). "You see the kids rallying around one another to get kids off the bench. In seventh grade the last thing you want to hear is more pressure from teachers or parents. They are able to close one ear to that. But when there's peer pressure to come to school and get off the bench, that's where we're seeing a lot of success in getting kids out of the mindset that going to school is not cool, that homework is not cool, that getting good grades is not cool." Based on the number of boy hands that regularly shoot up in KIPP classes, including among the older middle school boys who in another setting would succumb to the too-cool-for-school peer pressure, the KIPP formula appears to be working.

The other half of the KIPP formula is less complicated. What can appear to outsiders as smothering discipline at KIPP is actually smothering love. They don't allow students to slip quietly away and fail. At the end of class, teachers often urge students to call their home or cell numbers with any questions—unheard-of offers in most schools. "Kids need to know you care about them. They need to see you're invested in them," said Hayes. That caring trumps issues such as whether the teachers are male or female, black or white. And it trumps whether you're using teaching techniques geared toward boys. "Once they know you care about them they're going to do what you want," said Hayes. "They're going to perform in class, they're going to do their homework, and they're going to come to school. You're going to get the boys invested in school as well."

Davon has bought totally into KIPP. He knows the teachers care. He'll tell you all about the reading teacher with the phonics boost and the science teacher with the tutoring help. In true KIPPster style Davon has already picked out his target college, Howard University.

But can Davon, one of KIPP's weaker students being raised by a single mother (he says he has eight siblings and twenty-nine nieces and nephews) and exposed to abysmal public schooling in the earliest grades, recover enough to emerge from KIPP after eighth grade on a track leading him to Howard?

"He'll be close," answers Hayes. "I have no doubt he'll be successful in high school. What we've found is when our kids leave here and go to their public high school or a charter high school they're blowing those schools out of the water. Even our C-average students, when they leave us and go to a charter school down the street, are A students on the honor roll."

KIPP, the highest-scoring middle school in the district, places many of its students into elite private schools eager to find minority students who can handle their fast-paced academic challenges.

"Davon is probably where he needs to be to go to a public school," said Hayes, "but we'll keep pushing him."

Davon continued to receive extra help in reading through eighth grade there. On the eighth grade District of Columbia assessments he scored proficient in reading and advanced in math. Says KIPP principal Hayes, "His English teacher said he loved to read on his own and was one of the hardest-working kids in his class." Davon, she pointed out, came a long way from the day in third grade when Casey Fullerton found him crying because he couldn't read a worksheet asking him to fill in questions about himself.

Final update: In 2009 Davon was attending a Maryland public high school.

CONCLUSION: WHAT THESE SCHOOLS
HAVE THAT WORKS FOR BOYS

Of all the schools described above, I find the Frankford story most compelling. All the reforms at Frankford were designed to overcome the learning gaps found among the poor and minority students at Frankford—not gender gaps. Brittingham and the other teachers who got caught up in the revolution just wanted their students to have a shot at jobs beyond chucking, plucking, or landscaping. Amidst their improbable success they barely noticed they were producing equal outcomes in boys' and girls' performance. That was never the goal.

Years ago when Brittingham began her "Why not us?" campaign, many of the staffers didn't think it was possible to draw a line in the reading-and-math sand and say no child will fall below this line. Now they all believe it, and that's how Juan, who arrived here from Mexico City only two years ago speaking only Spanish, ended up reading at grade level in English at the end of fifth grade. That's how all the boys here succeed.

As with KIPP, there's no boys' strategy at Frankford, no sex-segregated classes, no special hands-on teaching techniques aimed at boys, no major recruitment drive to hire male teachers. Frankford has only two male teachers. So the question is, absent a boys' strategy, how did it end up doing right by the boys? And the answer is, pretty much the same way KIPP succeeds with no specific boys' strategy: When you refuse to let even a single student slide by, you end up helping boys the most because the boys are the big sliders.

The tricky question to answer is this: If KIPP can succeed with boys as a co-ed school, does Excellence Charter School really have to go to all-boys to succeed? Both schools are what I call "second-generation" charter schools. They are spinoffs of highly successful charter school operators, KIPP and Uncommon Schools, groups that have a roster of winning charter schools. So what makes Excellence work for boys, the fact that it's all-boys or the fact that it's part of the Uncommon Schools network? That's something that can't be answered with data, but an answer arises from observing the schools. What I saw in the physical education classes at Excellence were life lessons about competition and cooperation, one of scores of similar lessons infused into these boys every day. Even if only a handful of those lessons stick, the payoff down the road will be tremendous. I can guess that Sawicki could raise the test scores of those same boys while operating Excellence as a co-ed school, but he's offering these boys far more.

CHAPTER

7

Impediments to a Solution:
The Ideological Stalemate

IN MY YEARS as an editorial writer with *USA Today*, some of the most pleasant people I dealt with represented the major feminist groups: Kim Gandy from the National Organization for Women, Marcia Greenberger from the National Women's Law Center, and Emily Martin of the ACLU Women's Rights Project. Unfailingly, they were helpful, smart, and insightful. When it came to the issue of boys falling behind, however, some would write the most puzzling things. Gandy once wrote an op-ed for *USA Today* arguing that women dominating college campuses will trigger a conspiracy by males to diminish the value of a college degree. Wrote Gandy, "dominant groups find ways to protect their members."[1]

Constantly, I would ask myself: Why would such politically shrewd people go to such extreme lengths to diminish the problems boys are having in school, especially when at least half their female supporters have sons in school? There's no single answer, of course. And it's important to keep in mind that full gender equality in education for women is a relatively recent phenomenon, an achievement that didn't come easily. Protecting those gains is understandable.

In my travels, however, there's no evidence that measures taken to help boys hurt girls in any way. In fact, in interventions such as single-sex classrooms it appears that girls may benefit more than boys. There's something else at play here, and I think I have a sense of what that is. The head-in-the-sand position regarding boys appears to arise from a decade-old ideological clash instigated by Christina Hoff Sommers, who burst from her think tank world in 2000 with *The War Against Boys*.[2] Gaining an unusually wide audience through a series in *The Atlantic*, Sommers expertly laid out the case that boys, not girls, were the gender suffering in school. As explained briefly in Chapter 2, had she stuck with her solid argument that boys were in trouble and proposed solutions, it's possible the U.S. Department of Education might have launched a national investigation, identified the problems, and funded experiments to arrest the academic slide boys have experienced. Had that happened, the United States today could rank with Australia at the forefront of fashioning solutions to help boys.

But that didn't happen.

Instead, Sommers devoted most of her book to attacking feminists, blaming them for the gender gaps. Understandably, the feminists fought back, fingering Sommers as the tip of the spear of what they dubbed a "backlash" movement aimed at the hard-won gains of women. The attacks on Sommers were logical. After all, the book's subtitle was *How Misguided Feminism Is Harming Our Young Men.* Sommers's previous book, *Who Stole Feminism?: How Women Betrayed Women,*[3] was a direct attack on feminists. In the *War Against Boys*, Sommers simply rewarmed her first attacks, this time linking them to the boy troubles. Feminists proved very adept at fighting back, painting boy advocates as right wingers—essentially pasting Sommers's face on anyone who spoke out on behalf of boys.[4]

It appears, however, they may have been too successful.

As fresh data continues to confirm the worsening of the gender gaps, the naysayers find themselves playing the role right-wing spoilers played with global warming throughout the Bush presidency. Their diversion arguments, such as citing male/female wage differentials (an issue with debatable causes that has little relevance to the gender gaps) or pointing to male domination in corporate suites (true, but also not terribly relevant to the large-scale problems unfolding with boys) have become something akin to citing the occasional cool summer or the iceberg that's melting right on schedule. What global warming? The growing number of boys having academic problems in K–12 schools and the rising gender imbalances on college campuses become mere *inconvenient* facts best left unmentioned.

As a result of this standoff, the gender gaps became a *controversy,* something akin to a "he said–she said" shouting match on talk radio, which has pushed the issue to the policy sidelines. Just as it didn't take much to push climate change to the dark corner of the Bush agenda—any excuse would do—it didn't take a lot to push the boy troubles off the agenda of educators already smothered in a smorgasbord of reforms. But for someone like Kim Gandy, that's an odd position to paint yourself into. One day, possibly soon, thousands of mothers—mothers with sons struggling in school or daughters unable to find "marriageable mates"—will wonder why the gender gaps were ever considered *controversial*.

Sadly, the clash between the feminists and Sommers appears to be pointless. Today, Sommers says she never intended to *blame* feminists for the gender gaps, only for blocking interventions (a dubious claim, based on my reading of her book). In fact, she told me if granted a do-over she'd drop the inflammatory subtitle. It is obvious feminism has nothing to do with the boy troubles, Sommers told me. How else to explain the lopsided numbers of girls succeeding academically in Middle East countries that have not seen a feminist movement? She's right, but her conversion comes too late to head off an ideological clash that has left this issue politically untouchable. Key players in this issue, such as the female-dominated teachers unions, take their ideological cues from the major feminist groups. The federal Department of Education has yet to launch a study into the gender gaps. What possible reason, other than fear of controversy, could account for that? More evidence of the political freeze this has created comes from the series of major foundation reports in recent years warning of flat college graduation rates. The obvious low-hanging-fruit remedy is to bring male graduation rates even with female rates, and yet not a single one of those reports even mentioned the obvious. Again, there's no possible explanation for that save one—this bizarre political freeze arising from a pointless clash.

IS THERE A LOGICAL ARGUMENT THAT BOYS AREN'T IN TROUBLE?

No serious person would attempt to argue that black and Hispanic boys aren't in serious trouble, but there's plenty of room to debate whether the problem is limited to just those boys. The most prominent attempt to do that emerged in June 2006 when Sara Mead, a researcher for the newly launched education think tank Education Sector, published "The Truth About Boys and Girls,"[5] the first serious attempt to put facts, numbers, and charts behind the contention the gender gaps are overblown. Boys aren't doing *badly*, argued Mead. Girls are merely doing *better*. "In fact, with a few exceptions, American boys are scoring higher and achieving more than they ever have before. But girls have just improved their performance on some measures even faster."

Mead said it was intellectual curiosity, not ideology, that prompted her to investigate recent magazine articles about gender gaps,[6] and there's no reason to question that. Her research proved to be serendipitous. Given the swelling consensus at the time that boys were indeed in trouble, Mead's claim to the contrary proved to be the ideal man-bites-dog essay. On a news-dry Monday *The Washington Post* ran an admiring article about Mead's report on its front page. At the time I recall speculating whether the *Post* editors believed they had found the perfect riposte to *The New York Times,* which had been running a series of articles detailing the academic problems boys were experiencing. The *Post* story was just the beginning of the press coverage Mead's report received. "Widespread paranoia about a crisis for boys is basically overblown," Mead told CBS correspondent Wyatt Andrews[7] in a CBS broadcast about her report.

Mead says she was "shocked" by the attention the report received. "I've written on school choice issues, which are generally considered controversial, but nowhere near as controversial as this. . . . The thing I've realized since writing this is that gender issues just get a lot of attention." For anyone denying that boys are in trouble, the essay became an overnight cause célèbre. Its logic was clear and alluring: Girls are just doing *better*—the perfect explanation for why so many college campuses are sliding toward the 60–40 female-male ratios. That's cause for celebration, not alarm.

The obvious counter to Mead's argument lies in upper-income school districts such as Wilmette in suburban Chicago and Edina in suburban

Minneapolis, described in earlier chapters, where investigations turned up steep gender gaps among wealthy white students. But Mead is a serious and fair researcher; her arguments warrant serious consideration. The believability in Mead's argument lies in its impressive charts and graphs. Mead could tell you *exactly* how much the fourth grade boys gained in their reading scores. How can boys be in trouble if everything is getting better for them? Unmentioned, of course, was what any savvy Washington education policy analyst knows: It doesn't matter how fourth grade boys are doing. For more than a decade U.S. educators have been throwing their hands up in victory whenever test scores show big bumps up in fourth grade learners. Just wait until those kids are in eighth grade, they predicted: Those test scores will soar! By their senior year of high school those students will be vying with Singapore for best-in-the-world honors, we were told.

Any shoe-leather education reporter can tell you it hasn't played out that way. The longer American students stay in the classroom, the more they slump. Especially the boys. In the real world, the only snapshot that truly counts comes at age seventeen. At that age, boys (the ones still in school, that is) are set to either apply to college or move on to post–high school training. So while Mead's report briefly acknowledges that seventeen-year-old boys are faring terribly, especially in the reading and writing skills needed to survive either in college or job training, she sidesteps that to focus instead on the happier news at fourth grade. Problem is, nine-year-old boys don't apply to college.

In the spring of 2009 the federal Education Department released its new "national report card" on reading, and the pattern held. There were improvements, including among boys, in elementary and middle schools, but no change in high school, where the news remained dismal. Mead was right about one thing: When possible, boys and girls should be judged separately. Here's a quick summary of where the two sexes stand:

- *The Economy:* Men twenty-five years old and over who started high school but never finished have seen a 38 percent decline

in their real incomes since 1973. Those who never went beyond a high school degree experienced income declines of 26
percent. Those with some college saw their incomes decline
by 13 percent.[8]

■ *Education:* Overall, only 65 percent of boys graduate from
high school. Among Hispanic males, the rate is 49 percent.
Among African-American males, the rate is 48 percent.[9]

■ *Married Life:* In 2004, the share of middle-age American men
who have never been married stood at 16.4 percent. In 1977
that rate was 6.3 percent.

■ *Civic Engagement:* In the 2004 presidential election, 56.3 percent of eligible men voted in the election. That's a sharp drop
from 72 percent in 1964.

■ *Incarceration:* The ever-rising incarceration rate in the United
States over the past thirty years places it as the world's top
jailer, above Russia. In 2004 there were 1.3 million men in
state and federal prisons and another 646,807 men in local
jails.

There's not much to be complacent about in that list. Within the
education gaps, the reading difficulties are the most worrisome because
those are the very skills boys need to succeed in college. Among high
school seniors, 23 percent of the white sons of college-educated parents
scored "below basic" on federal reading tests.[10] So much for the suggestion
that this is a problem occurring among poor and minority boys. That slip
in literacy skills is occurring at exactly the time the world is revolving in
the direction of demanding ever more exacting literacy skills. That means
the flat literacy rate for middle school boys and a slight decline for high
school boys is far more serious than it appears.

The most appealing part of Mead's argument is that boys aren't doing
badly; it's just that girls are doing better. Depending on the age and

measure used, she's often right. For the most part, boys' performance is flat while girls keep improving. But given the economic realities of men needing post–high school academic credentials as much as women, flat falls short. The reality check remains two-year and four-year degrees earned, and by that measure men are in trouble.

HOW THIS POLITICAL STALEMATE PLAYS OUT LOCALLY: A STORY FROM MAINE

Anyone who wanders off Maine's stunning ocean-view roads to explore the backwoods towns understands why Mainers once jokingly debated whether to adorn their license plates with macaroni and cheese rather than lobsters. Apart from the mostly blue-blooded sailors who anchor in Camden and other scenic ports, Maine is a blue-collar state. In woodsy Maine, not a lot of lobster gets served for dinner.

Maine's reliance on the male-dominated industries of logging and commercial fishing would seemingly make this state one of the last to worry over the fate of its men. But just the opposite happened in 2004, when Maine became the first state to launch a task force aimed at rescuing its boys. The roots of that concern are found in out-of-the-way places such as Millinocket, a northern town well off the lobster and sailboat circuit. Millinocket is home to the Great Northern Paper Company, which in the 1980s employed more than four thousand workers in its mill there. By 2006 the mill was down to about five hundred workers.[11] Young people, especially the men, were fleeing the area in droves.[12]

The question Maine officials wanted answered was how to keep their nontourist economy alive and hang on to their young men. Economists studied the data and arrived at one solution: entice them into college. When Maine economists studied what happened to University of Maine graduates they found a striking number stayed in the state. But when

Maine officials looked at their college population, they found that women make up nearly two-thirds of the students on campuses at public colleges and universities. Those numbers, concluded state officials, meant the state risked losing even more young men. The key question became why so few Maine boys head off to college.

Poor academic achievement by boys in elementary, middle, and high school appeared to explain the poor college attendance rates for men, which prompted the Maine Department of Education in 2004 to launch the Task Force on Gender Achievement Differences. The forty-person task force set out to study why boys lagged behind in grades and test scores. The Maine report promised to be the first-ever statewide look into the gender gaps, a valuable resource that other states could draw from. But that never happened.

The story behind the report starts in 2000 when Duke Albanese, Maine's education commissioner at the time, noticed something odd while visiting Maine schools. Similar to most educators around the country, Albanese had trained himself to keep a special eye on girls' achievement, especially in math and science. That vigilance was a response to the numerous reports from the American Association of University Women and other groups about girls slipping into academic trouble.

But Albanese was seeing something different emerging. "It seemed like all the academic honors and recognitions were going to the young women. That led us to look at the test scores for boys in the fourth, eighth, and eleventh grades. And then we looked at the academic aspirations of the boys (how many planned to go to college). What we found was that the problems were shifting to the boys' side."

Maine educators talked about that discovery but never acted on it. Then, in 2003, Albanese stepped down as education commissioner and launched a new career at the Portland-based, education-focused Mitchell Institute, where he could take an even closer look at achievement gaps. Once again, he ran into the unresolved problem of boys slipping behind. "The ninth grade failure rates were absolutely dominated by young men.

And when we looked at college-going trends we saw trends that were very much distressful. Men were not starting college and those who did were not graduating. It became apparent that the problem was getting really big. I realized I had kind of dropped the ball in 2000."

This time Albanese was determined not to let the issue slip away. Using his foundation resources he pulled together a panel of Maine researchers and education experts to pool what knowledge there was about why boys were faltering in school. "We needed to do something." At that point the Maine Department of Education stepped in and asked to take over the project. "They had been hearing a lot of feedback on this," said Albanese, who happily turned the effort over to the state, which launched the Task Force on Gender Achievement Differences.

The task force, however, didn't last long in its original form before changing direction. The lead researcher appointed was Mary Madden, a University of Maine education professor who specializes in the development of adolescent girls. Madden appeared to have limited interest in a report that focused solely on boys. To say that boys are underachieving while girls are excelling is a "faulty comparison," Madden told *Portland Press Herald* reporter Kevin Wack. Early on, Madden and other like-minded members of the task force steered the project in a new direction. The shift was dramatic enough to prompt a renaming of the investigation to the Task Force on Gender Equity in Education. Overnight, the task force switched from studying boys' lapses in achievement to "equity" questions involving both sexes.

Equity sounds fair, but were girls in Maine truly in trouble? Madden says yes. "What happened is when we started to analyze the data by both gender and socioeconomic status it became clear to us that this was not just about boys," said Madden.[13] "It was too simplistic to try to look at boys as a whole group and girls as a whole group." For example, said Madden, looking just at boys would overlook the problems of low-income girls. In Maine, the school achievement dividing line is sharper along income lines than gender lines, said Madden. Thus, remedying the needs of poorer students, girls and boys, became one of the top priorities of the task force.

The next shift in direction arose after determining where the boys started going off track, which turned out to be middle school. Using a survey tool that measured "intrinsic motivation," which roughly translates into the desire to do better in school, the task force noted a sharp dropoff in the desire of middle school boys to do well in school. Given that the middle school years are when boys go through puberty, the task force quickly concluded that the problem lay in the psychological muddle boys endure in puberty. Seen this way, the issue becomes less about school achievement than confusion over issues of masculinity. That confusion, the theory holds, triggers academic problems.

Said Madden, "Something was going on at eighth grade, so the task force wanted to look at cultural issues of boys struggling with masculinity around that age. Does that play into whether it's cool to read, do well in school? What kind of pressure do they get, especially from their peers?" The path to solving the boy troubles, they concluded, lay in cracking the "boy code," that armor of tough-guyness that boys assume. That boy code, say psychologists such as William Pollack (see Chapter 5), results from parents who prematurely push their boys to become independent. That early separation from their mothers leaves them sullen, defensive, and unable to negotiate the stresses of school life. Thus, they flounder. Now the task force had an agenda that dovetailed neatly with the feminists who took on Sommers. Their position: If boy troubles exist at all beyond income and race, they involve machoism.

By the spring of 2006 a team of reporters from the *Portland Press Herald*, which had undertaken its own investigation of the boy problems in Maine, ran out of patience with the much-delayed task force report and filed a Freedom of Information Act request to force its release. When released, the sixty-nine-page report proved to be an embarrassment to the Maine Department of Education. Anyone willing to wade through the pages posted on the newspaper's website got a lesson in misguided political correctness. At times, the report's language more resembled an *Onion* spoof than a state investigation into education failures. Yes, the report conceded, women dominate the public college campuses in Maine, but that doesn't mean they have it easy. "Evidence suggests that women still experience classroom climates that are unfriendly and even hostile," the task force reported. What were the report authors referring to? Maine men, the authors informed us, are inclined to stare at Maine women. And staring can turn into "leering." Worse yet, said the investigators, are men who employ "jokes, or humor" to dominate a classroom.

When reading the report I tried to imagine being handed the task of convincing the unemployed men of Millinocket that their jobs are fading away because they look at pretty women. The oddest thing is how this ever ended up in what was supposed to be a serious task force report on boys falling behind in schools. I asked that question of Madden, who replied, "We were looking at barriers faced by both men and women."

The report authors conceded that Maine boys did appear to have a few academic problems. And they quickly settled on a cause for those problems that had nothing to do with the quality of teaching or the curriculum. What troubled boys was their own masculinity, concluded the report, referring to the "boy code" problems. *Portland Press Herald* reporter Beth Quimby, who along with Wack wrote the story based on the newspaper's own investigation of the boy problems in Maine, summarized the thrust of the report in this sentence: "It argues that if boys no longer aspired to tough guy ideals and girls moved beyond the compliant feminine ideal, both sexes would reach higher levels of academic achievement." I can only imagine what the men of Millinocket would think about being told to dial back their masculinity. Overdone masculinity was not the only villain identified in the report. The gender problem in Maine is not boys falling behind in school, said the report authors, but rather the press's writing about boys falling behind. "This report moves beyond catchy headlines and overly simplistic comparisons . . . the media leads us to believe that gender tells the story of school achievement," the report stated.

Madden and the other task force members couldn't be more wrong. School achievement is exactly what it's all about. Reform educators at the KIPP charter schools (see Chapter 6) aren't turning out boys who match girls in academic performance by addressing their masculinity issues. They are doing it by figuring out ways to teach all students to be competent readers and writers, including the boys. If the press doesn't play a role in pointing out that fact, who will? Certainly not the Task Force on Gender Equity in Education. The task force also blamed race and class for the education problems there, somehow overlooking the fact that Maine is nearly all white and mostly blue collar. Maine girls who are flourishing in the schools there come from the same families as the boys who are faltering.

Although the task force report got sidetracked, the *Portland Press Herald* went ahead with its investigation. Some of its findings include:[14]

- Twice as many boys as girls receive special education services.

- The gender gap starts at kindergarten but is most noticeable by fourth grade in reading and writing.[15] The gap widens through the grades, reaching its widest point in college.

- Boys are well behind in reading and writing on state tests; just 40 percent of eleventh grade boys met or exceeded standards, compared to 57 percent of girls.[16]

- Men earn only 38 percent of the bachelor's degrees awarded by Maine's public universities.[17] Male enrollment in 1972 was 55 percent.

- In the rankings of top ten high school seniors, girls outnumber boys by a two-to-one ratio.

- In Maine preschools, boys are four and a half times as likely to be expelled as girls.

- Maine men who enter college are less likely to graduate than women. At the University of Maine in Orono, the main cam-

pus, 44 percent of the male students graduate within six
years, compared to 59 percent of the women.[18]

There's little unique about those numbers.[19] Most states would find
the same thing if they made the effort to investigate. The Maine educators
quoted in the newspaper series were unanimous about their concern over
boys' achievement. "Everything has flip-flopped," said one female math
teacher. "Now these little boys are endangered." Said a high school counselor, "The picture, really even globally, is pretty gloomy for the male of
this species. The reality is I think we've got to really put some energy to
turning schools inside out so boys don't perceive them to be girls' places."

As the investigation by the *Portland Press Herald* revealed, the gender
gaps persist regardless of a family's income. The newspaper reporters di-
vided Maine's schools into two groups, wealthier and poorer. In each
group, girls' academic aspirations outstripped the boys' ambitions by the
same amount, ten percentage points.

In March 2007 the Maine Department of Education released its final
gender report—as quietly as possible. No press conference, no press release. No surprise there. Although the odder portions of the report were
dropped, the task force offered nothing to the folks in hard-pressed places
such as Millinocket. The first sentence of the introduction lays down an
attack on the "media" as the cause of all this misunderstanding about
boys not doing well. (In fact, I'm personally "honored" with a replication
of a headline from a 2004 *USA Today* editorial I wrote: "Pay closer attention: boys are struggling academically.")

That "struggle" is not what it seems, argue the authors over sixty
pages. Their "more in-depth understanding of the concept of gender"
leads them to conclude the press hysteria is all wrong. Gender, we're told,
is a minor player compared to race and class. The authors' struggle to
emphasize race in a state that's nearly all white injects some humor into
an otherwise tedious report.

Thomas Newkirk, an expert on boys and literacy who reviewed the report at my request, pointed to the same holes in the report. At the end of the report there's good, practical advice for teachers to encourage boys' literacy, said Newkirk, author of *Misreading Masculinity: Boys, Literacy, and Popular Culture*.[20] However, the discussion leading up to the suggestions is "muddled," said Newkirk, a professor of English at the University of New Hampshire. Pointing to performance differences between poor and wealthy students is pointing to the obvious. What's more difficult is explaining the gender differences within each class. In spite of drawing mostly from the middle and upper middle class, the University of Maine draws far more women than men. "In other words, even if you account for economic status, gender is a factor."

In the end, an ideal opportunity was squandered. "This was supposed to be a task force focused on boys' issues," said higher education consultant Tom Mortenson, who closely tracks the college gender gaps. "Instead its mission was diluted and the opportunity was missed to get out of our obsessive focus on girls' issues. . . . Maine is doing a fine job with its girls—it's the boys who need the most help now." A state like Maine is never going to revisit an issue that proved to be so contentious. For the folks in towns such as Millinocket worrying about losing their young men, that means waiting, and hoping, for the U.S. Department of Education to step in and investigate an issue that should have been properly investigated years earlier.

The International Story: Australians Struggle with the Boy Troubles

SITTING ACROSS FROM ME at Killara High School in the wealthy suburbs of Sydney is school principal Mark Carter and his boss Jane Simmons, the director of the North Shore Network of schools, which includes Killara and twenty-seven other schools, most of them blessed with similar favorable demographics. Killara is the highest performing public high school in all of New South Wales, which probably makes it one of the highest performing high schools in all of Australia.[1]

Simmons and Carter were explaining their plan to push the performance of Killara High School even higher. In recent years, Killara has been soaking up ever-higher percentages of younger children from nearby public elementary schools who might otherwise have gone to private schools. But now, Killara was outperforming one of those schools. Until four years ago, when Carter launched a drive to improve academic performance, Killara attracted just 30 percent of the children from those schools. The rest went to private schools. Now, in 2007, Killara was pulling in nearly 70 percent of those students, a point of pride for both Carter and Simmons.

Neither wants to see a reversal of that trend. Their latest plan to push excellence, which arose from the teachers at Killara, involves targeting boys, especially those coming into the middle school years. After scrubbing the data for grade trends, the teachers found the number of boys earning top grades had dropped dramatically. "There's a performance dip as students move from having just one teacher to having maybe ten teachers," said Carter. "Perhaps there's also a shift in [academic] expectations and not all students adjust. It's been observed that perhaps boys in particular don't adjust well."

As Carter and Simmons described the plan to target these young boys, I told them that in the United States such a plan would draw considerable controversy. First, critics would deny that well-to-do white and Asian boys (Killara has a large number of Asian immigrants) are having any school troubles. Then the reformers would be accused of discrimination for carrying out practices that would set back the success of girls. The two educators winced in amazement. "We're over that debate," said Carter. Simmons agreed. "That was a debate twenty years ago."

Based on my travels and interviews in Australia, the two educators are right. No one would suggest that Australia has found a solution for the boy troubles, but they are years ahead of the United States in pioneering solutions. In the beginning, there was contention about whether boys need help—contention that has not disappeared. But all parties here agree there's a problem and that it affects schools serving upper-income boys as well. That issue was wrapped up conclusively in 2003 after a federal "inquiry" into the boy troubles. Of course boys are having problems in school, concluded then education minister Brendan Nelson: "The problem is not that girls are doing better than boys—it is, instead, that boys are not doing as well as they once did." The economic realities in Australia and the United States don't differ. Boys need post–high school schooling as much as the girls, so even running in place falls short. That's what worried Nelson, and that's what should worry our education leaders.

What followed that inquiry in Australia were government-sponsored research and school experiments. In 2006 the government handed out eight hundred Success for Boys grants averaging $12,000[2] apiece to train teachers to adjust their teaching styles to reach more students, especially boys. In 2007, another eight hundred schools got grants. Most of the grants went to schools with the greatest needs, schools that educated high percentages of immigrants and children with Aboriginal backgrounds. Not all schools, however, fit that description. Two schools in Jane Simmons's upper-class North Shore Network sought and received grants. Aside from the training grants, all schools have access to thick, government-sponsored curriculum and teaching guides for reaching out to boys. The volume on boys' literacy is book-length.

But again, the real importance of what happened in Australia was the political truce: Yes, boys are obviously having trouble, so now let's figure out what to do about it in ways that don't set back the remarkable progress girls are making. One example of how that truce is paying off follows.

TREVOR BARMAN'S STORY: BLUE MOUNTAINS GRAMMAR SCHOOL, WENTWORTH FALLS

On this crisp March day, part of Australia's fall, the cricket and rugby fields at Blue Mountains Grammar School are so lush you can smell the fresh grass. As the trim, athletic students run through their after-school sports drills, it all looks so perfect, a picture suitable for framing. And then, from inside the gym, comes the staccato of fists slapping against leather. There, in a far corner of the gym, is the graphic design teacher with eight students, far scruffier than the rugby and cricket stars outdoors in the sun, decked out in fighting gear. These students, several with Aboriginal roots there on scholarship, are practicing their jabs and right crosses. As the students here at Blue Mountains most likely to lag academically or fall into discipline troubles, these boys had some aggression to work off.

Although there were no skateboards in sight at that moment, bad boy–style skateboarding is the true glue for this group. When the teacher came up with the idea of making a special effort to reach these boys, he discovered to his delight that they were all skateboarding fans. And when he chaperoned a trip for the boys to Sydney's hip skateboarding park, a two-hour train ride away, he won the hearts of these boys. "I try to give them support about what it is to be a young man," said the teacher, who was one of the "seed" teachers at Blue Mountains, a handful of teachers who sat through sessions with a professor/consultant who laid out the important points of the government's research into boys. He and other teachers then carried their lessons back to the rest of the Blue Mountains faculty.

That consultant, paid for by a grant from the federal government (in Australia, nonpublic schools also receive public funding), was only part of the push to help boys at Blue Mountains. It all started in 2003 when Trevor Barman was hired as a big-picture guy with a mandate to elevate academic quality there. Official title: deputy head–teaching and learning. Charged with turning this rural, nonselective private school (students vary from sons of doctors to daughters of truck mechanics) into one of Australia's top schools, Barman started his job working off a hunch he gleaned from his previous school. Boys, Barman had discovered at his previous school, were the weak link in the academic food chain. And when Barman started wielding his specially designed software, that's exactly what he found playing out at Blue Mountains.

Using Blue Mountains' own "benchmark" data—calculating how many students at the end of year ten meet their goals upon graduating at year twelve, he discovered something startling: While 75 percent of the girls made their benchmark goals, only 30 percent of the boys did the same. When he revealed that finding to the staff, the reaction was disbelief. "They had never seen data like this produced in a school before. Whereas some schools in Sydney might be part of this kind of data analysis, this was new for this school. Some didn't believe me." Barman, however, successfully pressed ahead with reforms, which in addition to training the "seed" staff included:

■ *Devising a special literacy intervention course for students lagging in those skills.* "The idea was to focus on kids requiring support in the first two years of high school so by the time they got into year nine they could go back into mainstream classes and require less support. . . . We tested kids prior to starting the program, in reading comprehension and spelling, put them on the program, and then retested them. All the students showed gains, some by as much as four years (of growth)."

- *Moving into a formal phonics program.* Part of the government grant program went toward purchasing phonics instruction materials from Lexia, a Massachusetts-based company that sells its materials worldwide. In the computer lab the Lexia materials to upgrade literacy skills worked on video game–style hand controllers the students enjoyed using.

- *Teaching the staff to break down learning tasks into "chunks" to reach boys with limited organizational skills.* "We encourage them to segment the material, break it into smaller chunks, and go through it at slower rates. Let the boys complete those tasks and make sure they experience success."

Another of those seed teachers I spoke with was a history teacher who became a passionate innovator of boy-friendly teaching techniques. Just handing students a large history project to complete dooms a third of the class to failure, she said. Most of those certain to fail are organizationally challenged boys who can't even imagine where to start. "Breaking things down seems like such an obvious thing to do, but it's not just a matter of breaking the material into pieces. You have to monitor the breaks and mentor the students along the way. Coming back to talk to the boys is absolutely necessary. With boys, you need to talk about it, you need to touch base." In her classes, those "chats" pegged to stages of the project became part of the grading process.

Those classroom changes, she said, bring modest but measurable success with boys. "From boys who didn't have the vocabulary to write intellectually I'm getting essays that at least target the question. Before, it was a scrappy piece of paper that didn't even address the question."

- *Starting single-sex classes in English, math, science, and history, at least one class per subject in each grade.* In some cases the single-sex classes aimed at boys lagging behind, but not always. In my interviews with students at Blue Mountains—interviews where the boys showed no shyness in criticizing anything that moved on campus—I heard nothing but positive reviews of the single-sex classes.

Blayne, 13, said he was a faltering student before being assigned to an all-boys class in year six (fifth grade in the United States). What made the difference, he said, was having a teacher who previously taught at an all-boys school. "He just knew how we'd react, what we'd like. We did more practical stuff, especially with math. It prepared me well for year seven when I won a silver [academic] award. I got excellent in nearly every subject."

"Girls," said Blayne, "just listen to lectures better than boys. We do all about the same in school until year five when boys get into the world of cricket and sport . . . that's a world of opportunity."

■ *Refusing substandard work from boys.* "This is one of the things we did that paid the biggest dividend," said Barman. "Now, when boys hand in sloppy work we actually follow up, which often means a phone call to the parents. And we ask them to redo the work to a satisfactory standard."

■ *Shifting the timing of parent-teacher conferences in the upper grades.* Traditionally, those conferences were scheduled three weeks after the exam period so the teacher and parents could discuss the results. Now the conferences come three weeks before the exam period. If the teachers sense problems the parents have an opportunity to get involved before the exam. But there's an even more important reason for the shift. This way, teachers have no choice but to get to know their students in ways other than as a score on an exam.

Boys, said the history teacher, need teachers to know something about their lives other than academic work. "Boys learn the teacher, and then they learn the subject. They want you to experience them as a whole person, not just a history student." At athletic events the boys always thank the teachers for coming to watch, she said. "And then they want to talk about it in class. . . . 'Did you see that shot I missed?' Girls couldn't care less if we watch their games, and they compartmentalize. . . . 'We're in history now, why would we want to talk about basketball?'"

Teachers can succeed with boys if they can re-create in the classroom the kind of teamwork boys find so alluring in sports, she said. "They have a role on the team, a sense of belonging. In the classroom, if they don't have a role they withdraw way over there." That simple shift increases the likelihood teachers will get to know the boys well enough to make them feel part of the class team.

DO THESE REFORMS HAVE A PAYOFF?

At Blue Mountains Grammar, Barman has set up software capable of tracking the progress of nearly every student, granting him a unique opportunity to evaluate and refine reforms. "We're gradually getting better every year. In three years we've managed to double the number of students scoring in the top 90th percentile or above [on the graduation index used in Australia that combines tests scores with grades]. We've gone from having 17 percent of our students in the top bracket to 30 percent." Most of those gains at Blue Mountains came from pushing boys from the middle to the top levels. "Before, we hardly had any boys up there. They were all down in the middle."

Targeting the boys at Blue Mountains Grammar continues to pay off: By the end of 2007 about 68 percent of the graduating boys met the school academic benchmarks (set at a level to make them eligible for the most competitive universities), up from 31 percent in 2002. That brings the boys roughly even with the girls.

In the rest of Australia, results from the boys' experiments are harder to measure. In most cases it's simply too soon to tell. These modest government attempts to tinker with the gender gaps are unlikely to put Australia on the map. Australia's importance in this issue lies elsewhere. By having the federal government stepping in to settle the issue of whether boys are actually having problems, and then funding experiments in boy-friendly teaching in both private and public schools, Australia opens up the possibility that individual educators such as Trevor Barman at Blue Mountains Grammar can pioneer changes that actually will make a difference. Those successes made a professional difference for Barman. In 2009 he was named head of school.

BEYOND AUSTRALIA: RAPID CHANGE AHEAD

Looking at the ultimate big picture—the world—men have all the advantages, at least men of a *certain* age from *certain* countries. Among those between the ages of 55 and 64, men are far more likely to be educated than women. In fact, among the thirty countries tracked by the Organisation for Economic Co-operation and Development, older women emerge as better educated in only three countries. That snapshot shifts dramatically, however, when you look at 25-to-34-year-olds. In that group, women are better educated than men in twenty of the thirty countries. Among those ten, only two countries, Switzerland and Turkey, showed significant differences favoring men.[3]

"In the OECD data, the United States is in the middle of the pack on most measurements of education gender gaps," said Tom Mortenson, a higher education consultant who has made gender gaps a specialty. "The gaps are more pronounced in the Scandinavian countries." On most international measurements of education gaps, women are well ahead of men, said Mortenson, with the exception of the sub-Saharan African countries. In the summer of 2006, Mortenson presented his data before a meeting of the European Access Network in Greece. "I told them what makes this a crisis is the loss of traditional male employment. Our economies are growing jobs but those jobs are in the service industry that requires higher education. For women, this brave new world has worked, but men are stuck where they were in the 1970s. The consensus response was that they were seeing the same trends in Europe and they didn't know what to do about it either."[4]

If Australia seems somehow too exotic to compare to the United States, instead consider Canada, the neighbor with the look-alike image many Canadians would prefer to shed. That won't happen with gender gaps, however. Canadian universities are experiencing a surge of females that mirrors what's happening in the United States. If anything, the Canadian gender gaps appear slightly larger, at least in some measurements. Canadian girls are more likely than the boys to show interest in their studies, find their classes relevant, and study hard: 46 percent of the high school boys surveyed there spend three hours or less per week on homework, compared to 29 percent of the girls. The relative disinterest Canadian boys show in school is reflected in the dropout figures. Among twenty-year-old Canadians, 15 percent of the men have failed to earn a high school degree, compared to 9 percent of the women.[5] Those trends are reflected in college enrollments, where men make up only 42 percent of the total enrollments.[6]

In 2007, two Canadian academics tried to make sense of the trends. In recent years the influx of foreign students and the rising percentage of graduate students have "raised the level of seriousness" of Canadian universities, write Clive Kean and Ken Coates.[7] "Young men, it appears, are less acclimatized to this new environment and less prepared to compete within it. More to the point, perhaps, the women's movement, combined with special attention paid to female success and learning styles at the elementary and high-school levels, is paying dividends. Large numbers of independent-minded females believe that their earning power will be significantly enhanced by obtaining university degrees with stellar grades attached." Men, by contrast, are less likely to take their studies seriously.

Said Marion Hannaford, the associate registrar at Thompson Rivers University in British Columbia, "When workshops or seminars on study skills, time management, exam-taking and the like are offered, it is rare to see a male student sign up voluntarily, and even fewer attend."[8]

At the University of Montreal, women make up 71 percent of the medical students, 63 percent of the law students, 80 percent of the optometry students, 64 percent of the dental students, and 56 percent of the management students. At McGill University, women make up 70 percent of the architecture students, 61 percent of the medical students, and 55 percent of the dental students.[9] The gender differences in maturity levels are stark, say the professors. "It's quite striking. Everyone has noticed it," said chemistry professor Heidi Muchall from Concordia University. The maturity differences are most noticeable in the youngest students, she said. The freshman women are far more likely than the men to do the reading and lab work.[10]

Jim Sentance, an associate professor of economics at the University of Prince Edward Island, speculates that shifts in teaching styles from lectures to collaborative learning could have something to do with the dramatic gender shifts seen there. "While the old learning style favored males, the new emphasis on discussion, participation, following directions, and meeting deadlines has moved us in the other direction. Boys don't see a lot of point in working hard on assignments when the grades are just shared out to others."

Educators in countries that have been targeting the problem of boys' underachievement say they have reasons to believe the trend lines are starting to shift. In Britain, for example, boys have nearly closed the math and science gap with the girls. The gaps in literacy, however, are proving to be more stubborn. Among fourteen-year-old girls there, 80 percent reached the expected "level 5" goals on English tests in 2006, compared to 65 percent of the boys.[11] Education officials there warned that level 5 represents the minimum skill level needed for further education, meaning that 35 percent of the boys were in danger. "A thorough grasp of reading and writing is essential for success in later life," said Nick Gibbs, the member of Parliament who oversees schools for the Conservatives. "The fact we are still concerned about the literacy levels of fourteen-year-olds is a sad indictment of educational standards in the country."[12]

My intention in this chapter is not to make this a book about worldwide boy troubles. Rather, it is to briefly point out that the problems we see in the United States are mirrored elsewhere. Countries such as England and Australia that are far ahead of the United States in examining the problem have reached the same conclusion: The world is becoming more verbal; boys aren't.

CHAPTER

9

Why These Gender Gaps Matter

IF YOU'RE A FATHER of daughters (like me) you've probably worried about drunk frat boys, leering professors, sexist bosses, and glass ceilings. It never occurred to me I'd end up worrying about my daughters' entering professions where a male frequenting the water cooler is rarely seen. Depending on the profession they choose, however, that could happen. Are women really taking over? Of course not. As National Organization for Women president Kim Gandy points out, men still run the Fortune 500 companies and dominate Congress. Why worry about the fate of men? Gandy has a point. The gender makeup of Congress matters, and while the steady rise in the number of elected women is cause for celebration, a quick glance at the membership of the U.S. Senate tells us there's a long way to go. And as everyone learned in the testosterone-charged Wall Street risk-taking excesses of the last decade, gender matters in corporate suites and boardrooms as well. But to stop there misses the day-to-day reality of where our daughters are more likely to work, which is not holding down a Senate seat or piloting General Electric, career paths that sociologists point out are more likely to be chosen by men than women.

In the real world, things are changing quickly. The changes start on college campuses, where life has already changed dramatically as women near the 60 percent mark, a point college admissions directors agree is a tipping point that changes campus life. Given the rising gender imbalances in college graduation rates, eventually those tipping points will emerge in white-collar workplaces, producing a mix of outcomes. Speeding all this along is the recession that broke out in 2008, where men suffered 80 percent of the job losses. At some point in 2009 women became the majority of the workforce.[1]

Many of those changes already are visible in our workplaces and personal lives. We just aren't accustomed to looking for them. It's the same phenomenon I experienced on college campuses that reached the tipping point where the balance of female students topped 60 percent. When walking around the campus of Virginia's James Madison University, for example, I didn't immediately notice this was a campus with far more women than men. Once I began looking for it, however, the imbalances were obvious. What follows are some observations on ways society is already changing—but you may not have noticed.

SOME WORKPLACES HAVE ALREADY CHANGED

Suppose your daughter realizes her fantasies to become a big-league television news producer and ends up in the Washington bureau of ABC News. There, her boss would be Robin Sproul, a thirty-year veteran of ABC News now serving as bureau chief. Sproul entered the business in local radio. She still remembers coming to Washington to interview for a job in the big time.[2] "When I went to interview here, the man stepping down told me I would get the job. I said great, but why, and he answered, 'Because they told me I had to hire a woman. You're the only one I know and I don't dislike you.'" The midday editorial meetings at that time consisted of Sproul and a room full of white men "who all smoked and all went to a bar for lunch."

On her way up the management ladder at ABC, Sproul was the first woman to hold all her positions. Her résumé of achieving so much as a woman makes the current situation at ABC and the other networks all the more puzzling. Instead of fighting for women to hold down still more key jobs, the dilemma today is more about finding competent men capable of working their way up from the bottom. At least three of every four applications to work at ABC News in Washington come from women, said Sproul. "It's very difficult for us to hire male applicants." The trend of men disappearing from the applicant pool first became noticeable to Sproul about ten years ago. Why? "I always feel like maybe the colleges have tipped or something (toward women), but also in a strange way I think salaries for journalism jobs, at least in broadcast journalism, have stayed low. They have not grown in relation. In a lot of cases girls are willing to take those low salaries and jump into it. For a lot of guys, this is not a ton of money."

Just to keep things in perspective, "desk assistant" starting jobs at ABC, where graduates from elite colleges answer phones and run support errands on shoots, start at around $30,000 a year. Those beginning jobs, however, can lead to producer jobs that pay six-figure salaries. The incentives for men seeking big paychecks remain. But winning those desk assistant jobs and then rising through the ranks requires a unique set of skills. Those from my generation will recall Radar O'Reilly from the long-running *MASH* television series. He was hyper-organized and knew how to sweet talk others into getting whatever the MASH unit needed. If you can imagine mixing Radar's fix-it skills with first-class writing abilities and winning phone manners, you've just described a desk assistant likely to win a producing job before she hits thirty. Remember Holly Hunter as a network producer in *Broadcast News*, micromanaging the Manhattan cab driver on how to sidestep traffic backups? That was reality.

I use "she" because, as all the networks are discovering, those talents are found in far more women than men. Even at the senior producer level at ABC it's not uncommon to walk into a meeting and see only one male face. "We'll joke about it," said Sproul, "and tell him, 'You're our token guy.'" Few people know about these gender shifts in the television business because that's not what they see on the screen, where there's generally an even mix of male and female correspondents. But don't be fooled by on-air appearances. Women, not men, make up the backbones of those broadcasts.

At the local level, the gender imbalances may be more pronounced. As local anchors, women reached parity with men in the early 1990s, the *Washington Post* reported.[3] By 2005 the percentage of female anchors rose to 57 percent, with many local shows abandoning the male-female standard and instead going with two women as anchors. At the backroom level, the gender divide is more dramatic, with two of every three news producer jobs held by women.[4] The unimpressive salaries paid at the local TV level may explain part of the gender shifts taking place there. But it's also clear that women are simply better at the job.

I'm guessing that as viewers of television news, you haven't noticed these changes. Given that the most dramatic shifts have taken place behind the cameras, that's understandable. But similar unnoticed changes are taking place in doctors' offices, insurance firms, and public relations companies. Often, the shifts bring unexpected consequences. Consider the television market, where every year the viewers tend to skew a little more to the female side. Is that a result of women dominating all but the very upper tier of the broadcasting industry? "I think it's going to be problematic," said broadcast consultant Jerry Gumbert.[5] "The average viewer wants balance, both in the kinds of stories that get reported and who appears on camera. They want to see a reflection of their community. Once that balance gets pushed too far in one direction, then the editorial decision making will change significantly, too. It can't help not to, because what interests men and women is different."

Sproul agrees there's a potential danger. The surge in female television news producers helped invigorate the stagnating evening news shows that had been run by men, she said. But the fact that women now dominate the business could trigger the same problems experienced when men ran everything. Editorial meetings where the news decisions are made need a diversity of perspectives, she said. "You wouldn't want an all-female group. You need to think the way a mixed audience thinks."

BEYOND NEWSROOMS

Some of the most compelling gender shifts are taking place in the least likely fields. In June 2009 *The Washington Post* reported on the surprising (to that author, at least) number of female FBI agents leading major white-collar crimes units. In the Baltimore field office, a third of the roughly 200 agents are female. Nationally, female agents now number about 2,500, or nearly 20 percent of the FBI force, which has long held the reputation as a male-only redoubt.[6]

The best indicators of the new economic realities are unfolding in urban areas, where jobs requiring higher levels of education are more likely to be located. In New York City for example, the gender salary gap favoring men among those with a college education has been narrowing.[7] And among all young workers between 21 and 30, regardless of education levels, women outearn men. Women working full time earned 117 percent of men's wages, according to a study released in 2007 by Queens College demographer Andrew Beveridge.[8] Those wage discrepancies favoring women held across the city despite the considerable number of high-salaried Wall Street jobs held disproportionately by men. That same trend was playing out in several large cities such as Los Angeles and Dallas. In Dallas, women made 120 percent of what men made. Those numbers appear to reflect the overall education advantage women enjoy.[9]

The trend documented by Beveridge in 2007 is likely to continue as more professions, such as news reporting and producing, swing female. Another example is clinical psychology, where more than 70 percent of the Ph.D.s granted each year are earned by women. The changes will continue to be gradual, rather than dramatic, which makes them less visible.

Some professions, ranging from plumbing to investment banking, are unlikely to see any dramatic changes in gender composition. Men are likely to continue seeking those out in greater numbers. Beyond wage shifts, the impacts from the education imbalances favoring women are a matter of speculation. Back in the days when men dominated the clinical psychology profession, it was fair to ask how those male psychologists would divine the female mind. Today, it's equally fair to ask the same question about the female clinical psychologists.

What worries CEOs from companies such as Intel that are deeply immersed in the international economy, however, is this: What happens in critical fields such as engineering, typically chosen by more men than women, when the pool of men entering college shrinks? These CEOs don't care about hiring men versus women; their concern is finding technically literate innovators. CEOs from tech companies are adept at reading numbers, and the numbers from the U.S. Department of Education that catch their attention are these: Over the next decade, the number of women with graduate degrees will grow by 16 percent, compared to a growth of 1.3 percent for men. To business executives, that means working harder to recruit and promote women who pursue technical fields, including those who take time off to raise a family. From their perspective, however, the more challenging problem is luring more women into the fields from which they want to hire. Over the past fifteen years, high schools have made dramatic improvements in the job of ensuring that young women are adequately prepared in math and science. As measured by who performs well in advanced placement science and math courses, girls more than equal boys. College, however, has turned out to be a different story, with many young women who in high school showed great potential for technical fields choosing other majors in college. That trend is playing out even in California, home to many of the nation's largest high-tech corporations. As California's public university system grew, a trend explained mostly by an increase in women, the number of engineering bachelor's degrees fell.[10]

In many nontech professions, a shift in favor of females is likely to play out with mixed results. In medicine, everyone is likely to benefit from less-gruff bedside manners. But as women move past the 50 percent mark in medical school, existing gender differences are likely to become even more apparent. Female doctors are also less likely to work the longer hours put in by most male doctors. A third of female doctors work part time, compared with 4 percent of male doctors. Plus, female doctors are choosing pediatrics and obstetrics as medical specialties, where they make up two-thirds of the medical workforce.[11] Given the projected shortage of physicians, will those specialties be as relevant in an aging population? Already, a similar issue is playing out with veterinarians, a field now heavily dominated by women. Partly as a result of female vets preferring to take care of cats and dogs rather than cows, farmers are suffering from a shortage of large-animal vets. Some cattle that in years past could have been saved by a quick medical intervention are now converted into beef.[12]

Women moving into politics appears to be a clear win-win proposition, with the 2008 elections adding to the impressive numbers female politicians posted in the 2006 midterm elections. But as these changing gender roles in the workforce are noted, and in most cases celebrated, it is also useful to raise the possibility of unseen impacts. Who would have anticipated a shortage of large-animal vets?

THE GENDER PAY GAP

With more women than men earning bachelor's degrees, more women than men earning graduate degrees, and a higher percentage of jobs requiring an advanced education, then why do college-educated women still earn only 89 percent of what college-educated men earn? The answer is a complex mix of what men and women study in college, what jobs they pursue, the career paths within those jobs, and, finally, old-fashioned discrimination. In some pay inequity cases where actual discrimination is ruled out, economists speculate there may be a gender difference in negotiating. Part of that gap remains an unsolved mystery. Regardless, this is an issue that can't be ignored. One comment I often hear from women about men disappearing from some white-collar jobs is: Before we worry about men let's solve the gender gap in pay that disfavors women. Important point, but is it relevant to the gender gaps? If some businesses truly do pay men more than women for the same job, we should applaud as lawsuits bring offenders to their knees. Most economists, however, say discrimination has little to do with the pay gap. The big drivers behind the gaps, they say, are women making different career decisions. At elite law firms, talented women are far more likely than men to turn down partnership tracks, mostly to avoid the crushing hours demanded of them. At Harvard University, women are increasingly likely to turn down tenured positions.[13]

To me, the wage gap issue mostly reflects the past rather than the future, as a 2009 study of pay gaps in the federal government indicated.[14] Speaking as the father of two daughters sensitive to any workplace slights against women, that's a relief. What the future appears to promise is a shift in gender power coming from women earning more and married women having more say about how dual incomes are spent. That should come as no surprise: About 44 percent of all household income is earned by women and about a quarter of wives earn more than their husbands.[15] The impacts of these gender earnings shifts range from the trivial to the profound. An example from the trivial side of the ledger: One reason for the sharp slide in the number of private pilots, we're told, is wives and mothers exercising their veto power. Stay-at-home moms were less likely to object to their husbands taking off for expensive and time-consuming flying lessons, Phil Boyer, president of the Aircraft Owners and Pilots Association, told *The New York Times*. That has changed. Today, she's more likely to say, "You are not. That's your day to take Johnny to the soccer game, and what the heck are you doing spending our hard-earned money on flying lessons?"[16]

A RISE IN CAMPUS FRICTIONS

Given the gender imbalances on college campuses, anyone looking for outbreaks of gender conflict would look first to those campuses and recall the famous flap sparked by former Harvard president Lawrence Summers over female scientists. The price Summers paid for his public musings about intrinsic shortcomings women might have in math and sciences was his job. Summers resigned in February 2006.

Over time, however, Summers's foot-in-mouth incident is likely to fade in importance. There are far bigger issues swelling up on college campuses. One clue to those future conflicts was revealed in October 2006 when the American Association of University Professors released charts laying out an obvious irony: Although female students dominate universities, female professors lag far behind. On some campuses, two out of every three degree earners are women. But overall, the percentage of full professors who are women hovers at 24 percent.[17] The report delves into the details of the inequity, finding that women faculty members earn less and are far more likely to get stuck with the "instructor" or "associate" positions that force them to lecture at four different colleges. Overall, they hold less than a third of the tenured positions. The question of why this has not bubbled up into a national fight is intriguing.

In the academic realm of the sciences, where Summers famously blundered, the potential for conflict is even greater. At the top universities, only about 15 percent of the full professors in social, behavioral, or life sciences are women, "and these are the only fields in science and engineering where the proportion of women reaches into the double digits," according to a report from the National Academy of Sciences.[18] "There are circles of communities of engagement where women are by and large not included," said Kathleen Matthews, dean of natural sciences at Rice University.[19] These inequities at the professorship level persist even though women now make up more than half of the medical degree earners in the United States and are pushing to that threshold in disciplines such as biology and mathematics.

When it comes to college governance, the numbers for female leaders lag far behind the undergraduate realities. A survey of four-year colleges and universities released in January 2009 found that between 1981 and 2007 the percentage of trustees who are women rose only from 20 percent to 31 percent. During that same period, the percentage of women serving on college boards rose from 10 percent to 18 percent. The elite universities are no exception. In 1994, when Judith Rodin became the University of Pennsylvania's first female president, she was only the ninth woman to serve on that board's Executive Committee.[20]

Professorships, presidents, and board members are not the only likely gender flashpoints on campuses. Despite the ever-growing number of female students and the gains women athletes have made under Title IX, the number of women who run college-level sports programs continues to lag.[21] Sports may prove to be campus flashpoints with students, as well. I visited James Madison University in Harrisonburg, Virginia, shortly after the university announced it would cut teams to come into Title IX compliance. The problem there lay in the numbers: James Madison is 61 percent female, but women made up only about half the athletes. After the changes take place, women will make up 62 percent of the varsity teams.[22] While at JMU I stopped by to visit with male swimmers as they gathered for a grim practice. Some of them had transferred to JMU after the swim teams at their previous schools had been disbanded for the same reason. To a swimmer, they all blamed Title IX.

Title IX emerged as a broad villain on the campus, not just among the athletes. Shortly after my visit, JMU students rallied in protest both at the university and at the U.S. Department of Education in Washington. In the protest in downtown Washington, D.C., JMU students sang the school fight song and chanted "save our sports." After meeting with an assistant to the secretary, the students ran around the building and then departed for a five-mile run through Washington.[23] Said JMU sophomore class officer Tara Rife, "Hopefully the rallies against Title IX will help the Department of Education realize that Title IX is an outdated law and rather than giving opportunities for women to compete . . . it's actually discriminating against men."[24] The university did little to discourage the idea that Title IX was the villain. Said a JMU spokesman, "JMU students don't take things lying down; they're not apathetic. The fact that they took their message to Washington makes us proud."

To counter the impression that Title IX was at fault, leaders of the Women's Sports Foundation, National Women's Law Center, and other groups held a teleconference to point the finger at JMU, which they said had compliance options other than cutting sports teams. "By blaming Title IX, JMU's administration is not only misdirecting student anger, but is unnecessarily undermining one of the nation's most successful civil rights laws," said Lisa Maatz, director of public policy and government relations for the American Association of University Women. JMU had other options, including trimming its football and basketball programs, said the leaders. "JMU's decision to cut [sports teams] was purely financial and philosophical," said Donna Lopiano, CEO of the Women's Sports Foundation. "JMU has decided to join the Division I arms race in football and basketball."

At this point, students could pick their villains, choosing among Title IX, football, or basketball. Notice what went unmentioned by both sides: JMU got itself into this jam because its female student population had crept past the 60 percent threshold, which has nothing to do with either Title IX or football. In the coming years, more colleges will pass that threshold and the outcome is likely to be the same: more campus conflict.

Fights over faculty appointments and sports teams aren't the only likely impacts of these gender imbalances. Based on my tours of campuses where gender imbalances reached the 60–40 threshold, most of the discussion was about campus social life. On the surface, it would seem logical that if women dominate colleges and universities, then life for female students should improve. In many ways that is true. On campuses I visited where the female students made up more than 60 percent of the student body, women ran most of the university activities and dominated student government. Interpersonal relationships, however, were a different matter. And that's a hot topic. A commentary I wrote for the *Chronicle of Higher Education* describing how campus social life gets skewed by gender gaps drew more than 14,000 downloads on my website/blog, whyboysfail .com.[25] The piece described what social scientists dub the "operational sex ratio"—what transpires when sex ratios become unbalanced among either animals or humans. When this plays out on college campuses it isn't pretty and mostly involves young men taking advantage of their relative scarcity, drawing the resentment of the women. In April 2009 I was amused to see that *Playboy*'s attempt to identify the nation's top ten party schools used a "bikini index" to arrive at its "scientific" conclusion. On the bikini list: weather, cheerleaders, and . . . female-to-male student ratio. From *Playboy*'s male readership perspective, that's entirely logical. From a female perspective, those might be campuses to avoid.

MARRIAGEABLE MATES

In 2006 country singer Trace Adkins turned out a hit song, "Ladies Love Country Boys," that must have warmed the hearts of every country boy out there. According to Adkins, parents' attempts to make their daughters successful and independent come undone when they meet a country boy and cast aside their high-powered careers. Turns out, according to Adkins, that our hard-charging daughters yearn for a good-ol'-boy with a pickup truck and farmer's tan. Adkins got part of it right. Parents do pressure their daughters more than their sons to succeed in school. And girls fulfill those wishes, pulling down most of the A's handed out by teachers. Not only do they go on to college in far greater numbers than the boys, but they earn better grades and are more likely to graduate.

That leaves only one thing Adkins got wrong. But it's a big thing. Our highly educated daughters don't want to marry country boys. Or, to be more precise, women prefer not to "marry down," social scientists agree. Men, by contrast, have fewer problems with marrying down. They're more open to marrying Daisy Mae, which is one of the many mysteries of matchmaking. Researchers come up with some elaborate theories to explain this gender difference. My favorite is the theory that men are paranoid and believe that "marrying down" is a hedge against infidelity, a way of ensuring that offspring are genetically related to them. Whatever the reason for the differences in marrying preferences, it's real and has become a player in the out-of-kilter gender world our children are entering. If two of every three college graduates are female, that leaves a shortage of college-educated men from which our daughters can choose.

To social scientists, that's dubbed the "marriageable mate" dilemma. And while most of the marriageable mate discussion centers on women unable to find a similarly educated partner, men are equally affected. I hadn't thought much about the second part of that dilemma until the *New York Times* ran a perceptive article[26] laying out the problem from the male perspective. Men lacking a college degree are increasingly less likely to get married, the reporters concluded. Twenty-five years ago, only 8 percent of men with less than four years of college between the ages of 40 and 44 had never married. By 2006 that figure had jumped to 18 percent. While some of those men are unwilling to marry, a fair number simply can't find a woman willing to marry them.

"Men don't marry because women like myself don't need to rely on them," said Shenia Rudolph, a divorced mother from the Bronx. Any marriageable mate, said Rudolph, would "have to have a job; you have to be educated; you have to have your own apartment and a car. Both have to contribute something."[27] Driving this phenomenon, said Valerie Oppenheimer, professor emeritus of sociology at the University of California, Los Angeles, are rapid changes in education and workplace fortunes for men. "In the past guys could drop out of school after finishing high school, or even without finishing, and go into a factory and get a steady job with benefits. But there has been deterioration in young men's economic position, and women are hesitant to marry a man who is likely to be an economic dependent." So much for Trace Adkins's wishful thinking that female big-city lawyers want to marry country boys.

In African-American neighborhoods, the marriageable mate issue is not new but remains painful. Given the sharp education differences, with twice as many black women in college, that's not surprising. Among blacks, the issue's visibility has risen enough to spill over into movies with crossover appeal. The 2006 movie *Something New*, starring Sanaa Lathan and Simon Baker, tells the story of a hard-charging black female executive who falls in love with a laid-back, white landscaper. When the two stars appeared on Oprah's television show, Oprah was quick to cite the dismal marriage numbers among black women and laud the movie for its trend-setting potential. Expanding the universe of acceptable marriageable mates, both by race and socioeconomic standing, would expand the pool greatly. "The world is a great big, wide place where there's possibilities to love lots of different people," said Oprah. "But that's why [*Something New*] is so great—because it's a full-circle moment in opening your heart to the possibilities."

The social and personal side of gender imbalances have spilled into the public view in recent years. In Asia, the rising social status of women coupled with the falling numbers of marriage-age women (the result of couples using sex-screening technology to choose sons, usually for economic reasons) has fueled an international marriage market. In South Korea, blue-collar men finding few Korean women interested in marrying them have turned to marriage brokers to arrange matches with poor Vietnamese girls, usually from rural areas. What's striking is the speed of this trend.[28] "Nowadays, Korean women have higher standards," said Lee Eun-tae, the owner of Interwedding, an agency that matches Korean bachelors with brides from other countries. "If a man has only a high school degree, or lives with his mother, or works only at a small- or medium-size company, or is short or older, or lives in the countryside, he'll find it very difficult to marry in Korea."[29]

In China, sex screening (or worse, infanticide) has created what may be the most gender imbalanced country in the world. As of 2009 China had 32 million more boys than girls under the age of twenty.[30] "Chinese commentators fear the effect on public order, painting a picture of bands of testosterone-crazed youths roaming the countryside, raising hell," reported *The Economist*.[31] By comparison with China or South Korea, the impacts of the education gender imbalances in the United States appear modest, except in the African-American community. Already, however, the marriageable mate issue has begun to seep into the white world.

FAILURE TO LAUNCH

The marriageable mate issue gets intertwined with the "failure to launch" syndrome, the increasing reluctance by young men to pursue traditional marriage and career paths. Some of "failure to launch" is tied to the increasing education gap between men and women, but other factors come into play as well, such as the "Guyland" values described in Chapter 5. Either way, women end up with fewer marriageable mates. The dilemma was nicely illustrated in the romantic comedy *Failure to Launch*, released in March 2006. The movie starred Matthew McConaughey as a thirty-five-year-old guy living at home with his parents. The parents want to see their son move on with his life (and move out of their house), so they hire Sarah Jessica Parker as a motivation consultant who pretends to fall in love with McConaughey as a ploy to pry him out of the house.

Author Dr. Leonard Sax was struck by how the movie captured what he saw in his own practice—scores of young men disinclined to launch themselves in life. Sax wrote about that in an op-ed for *The Washington Post*:[32] "This phenomenon cuts across all demographics. You'll find it in families both rich and poor; black, white, Asian and Hispanic; urban, suburban and rural." Girls, Sax wrote, are generally achieving their goals in life while too many young men remain directionless. In his subsequent book, *Boys Adrift*,[33] Sax tells about the *Post*'s inviting him to participate in an online chat. "The chat line was open for just sixty minutes. Staffers at the paper shut the line down after 395 posts, which they told me was more than double the previous record for a sixty-minute chat of 170 posts."

Why so popular a topic? Because it touches so many people, Sax argues in his book. Over the past decade, the proportion of young women 18 to 35 living at home with parents or relatives has remained constant, while the proportion of young men doing the same has doubled, said Sax. As Sax points out, "failure to launch" is one more reason we can expect to see rising rates of unmarried women, including college-educated white women, having children. Unmarried mothers accounted for roughly 5 percent of births in 1960; as of 2009 they are bearing nearly 40 percent of the nation's babies.[34]

Those are the reasons why we should care about the growing gender imbalances disfavoring boys. The final question becomes: What can we do about it?

CHAPTER

10

Actions That Need to Be Taken

IN MY YEARS of reporting on this issue, I've come across parents who insisted on an equal education for their sons; teachers who took charge of the problem and produced good results for their male students; principals who insisted on reshaping their schools to give boys a fair shake; and even governments willing to probe the issue (unfortunately, not in the United States). Adding up all those positives amounts to a take-action list, which includes the following actions.

LAUNCH AN AUSTRALIAN-STYLE FEDERAL INQUIRY (AND BASE THE RATIONALE ON GLOBAL COMPETITIVENESS)

In April 2009, *New York Times* columnist Tom Friedman delivered the latest indictment of the U.S. education system:

> Speaking of financial crises and how they can expose weak companies and weak countries, Warren Buffett once famously quipped that "only when the tide goes out do you find out who is not wearing a bathing suit." So true. But what's really unnerving is that America appears to be one of those countries that has been swimming buck naked—in more ways than one.
>
> Credit bubbles are like the tide. They can cover up a lot of rot. In our case, the excess consumer demand and jobs created by our credit and housing bubbles have masked not only our weaknesses in manufacturing and other economic fundamentals, but something worse: how far we have fallen behind in K–12 education and how much it is now costing us. That is the conclusion I drew from a new

study by the consulting firm McKinsey, entitled "The Economic Impact of the Achievement Gap in America's Schools."

Just a quick review: In the 1950s and 1960s, the U.S. dominated the world in K–12 education. We also dominated economically. In the 1970s and 1980s, we still had a lead, albeit smaller, in educating our population through secondary school, and America continued to lead the world economically, albeit with other big economies, like China, closing in. Today, we have fallen behind in both per capita high school graduates and their quality. Consequences to follow.

For instance, in the 2006 Program for International Student Assessment that measured the applied learning and problem-solving skills of 15-year-olds in 30 industrialized countries, the U.S. ranked 25th out of the 30 in math and 24th in science. That put our average youth on par with those from Portugal and the Slovak Republic, "rather than with students in countries that are more relevant competitors for service-sector and high-value jobs, like Canada, the Netherlands, Korea, and Australia," McKinsey noted.

Actually, our fourth-graders compare well on such global tests with, say, Singapore. But our high school kids really lag, which means that "the longer American children are in school, the worse they perform compared to their international peers," said McKinsey.

Parents in leafy middle-class suburbs don't realize they are sending their children to schools that aren't preparing them for the new world economy, the report warned. The report may have shocked some new to the education reform debate, but in truth reports like that have been raining down for several years. Hardly a month goes by without another major foundation or advocacy group reminding us of the perils this country faces if we don't send more of our students to college and ensure they emerge with degrees. The international Organisation for Economic Cooperation and Development warns that the United States is slipping fast in international rankings: Among those 25 to 34 years old, the United States ranks no better than tenth in higher education attainment. More striking was the "survival rate," the measurement of the number of students who enroll in college who end up graduating. There, the United States ranks at the bottom of the developed world. The "Gathering Storm" report from the National Academies urged dramatic steps to reverse the education gap.[1]

Visit the websites of foundations such as Gates, Lumina, or Broad and they all deliver the same message: The United States has an education canary in the mine that's being ignored. The U.S. Chamber of Commerce and Business Roundtable have been warning us of this for years.

Here's what not a single one of those reports was forthcoming enough to admit: These education numbers look bad primarily because the schools are failing *boys*. For the most part, the awful high school graduation numbers are driven by boys, not girls. The flat college enrollment rates are driven by gender. And the lackluster college graduation rates—those who actually earn a diploma within six years after enrolling as freshmen—are due primarily to men floundering in college. What should be of special interest to national business leaders is the impact of having this particular group, males, fade as learners. Because men and women tend to choose different college majors, any shift in campus gender balances brings changes in economic competitiveness. Again, the numbers from California: As the public university population swelled, due mostly to more women graduating, the number of bachelor's degrees in engineering shrank.

The longer we wait to tackle the boy troubles, the bigger the problem we'll have, warns University of Alaska professor Judith Kleinfeld, who launched the Boys Project, an advocacy group. "Boys are in trouble in critical academic areas no matter what their income levels. The nation needs to address the gender gap immediately before boys decide that school is an arena where the girls, but not boys succeed, and the boys decide they 'do not care' and withdraw from the competition. The situation is critical. At the moment, both boys and girls explain the gender gaps by saying boys are lazy and immature. The danger is that the boys will internalize this negative stereotype and it will become a self-fulfilling prophecy. The nation still has the opportunity to prevent this from happening and losing the talents of many young men, but we must act and act now."

Only one action, a federal probe into the boy troubles, will send those educators, legislators, think tankers, and business leaders in the right direction. As Australia discovered, it's all about the boys. Any strategy designed to boost global competitiveness that ignores the boys problem ends up ignoring the obvious solution. Currently, men make up only about 42 percent of those earning bachelor's degrees. There's no evidence that men need college any less than women do. Boosting that rate closer to 50 percent, where it belongs, amounts to going after achievable solutions.

And yet not a single one of those groups suggests looking at the college gender gap as a solution. How can that be? As explained in Chapter 7, the gender gaps have become a *controversy*, something to be avoided. In some circles, discussing the boy troubles is akin to launching into an abortion debate at the Thanksgiving table. This is silly. A quick glance at the college numbers tells us we have an issue that can't be avoided. The only way to move beyond the controversy is a federal inquiry, exactly what the Australians did. President Obama, with his sensitivity to the plight of black boys, is the ideal president to launch the research.

Obama needs to order the U.S. Department of Education to turn out the kind of report British education authorities released in the summer of 2009, a fact-driven analysis of actual gender learning differences. Would it hurt anyone to discover the truth? According to *The Independent*, the British discovered "a 20 percentage point gap . . . emerging in writing ability, with 74 percent of girls able to use writing for a variety of purposes, compared with just 54 percent of boys." Anne Mountford of the children's charity 4Children says, "The economy is moving much more toward communications skills and girls seem to be tearing ahead. If we don't act, boys won't be job-ready for the world that is coming."[2]

This is not a matter of settling scores. Rather, it is a matter of doing right by our sons and teachers looking for what works for boys. In the introduction I told you the story of Paul Ortiz, who was forced to patch together a boy-friendly classroom curriculum from bits and pieces gleaned from TV documentaries and magazine articles. "It's scary at times," Ortiz told me as he worried about doing the wrong thing for either the boys or girls in his class. But he knew he had to do something. What Ortiz and others like him deserve is federal research to pinpoint the source of the problem and fund experimental remedies.

TURN BOYS INTO EARLY READERS

In the late 1990s children's author Jon Scieszka was beginning to make his way in the publishing world with boy-friendly books such as *The Stinky Cheese Man and Other Fairly Stupid Stories*[3] and *The True Story of the 3 Little Pigs!*[4] Taking notice was an up-and-coming New York City principal destined to become deputy chancellor and top instructional leader for the New York schools. She invited Scieszka to her school to read stories to the children and took great interest in Scieszka's pleas to do more to elevate the literacy abilities of boys. As the principal worked her way to the top, she kept those lessons in mind. Given the dismal academic performance and graduation rate of boys in the system, it was a lesson hard to miss.

In 2004 when this principal was appointed by Chancellor Joel Klein to the top instructional post, she remembered what Scieszka had taught her about the gender gaps and reached out to him for help. The timing was fortuitous. Not only was Scieszka's Guys Read website attracting attention but he had just made a video and brochure aimed at both students and teachers about getting boys to read. Scieszka and the children's book publisher that sponsored the video sat down with school officials to map out a plan to boost boys' literacy skills. The publisher volunteered to underwrite the expense of shipping the video to every third and fifth grade class in the city.

"Part of it was me, speaking to kids in an animated, *South Park* kind of style. I wanted to get kids talking about boys reading in a 'let's talk about it' kind of style. It was a conversation starter." The balance of the video was aimed at teachers, offering ideas to get more boys interested in reading. "They were wildly excited," recalls Scieszka, "saying, 'Yeah, let's make this happen.' The job of making all this happen ended up on the lap of an informal committee of assistants. And then the wheels started falling off."

Scieszka recalls the first time he realized his idea was in trouble. "I was in a meeting and this assistant to the assistant said, 'We need to do something for the girls, too. We don't want to leave them out. Why can't it be about boys and girls reading?' and I replied, 'Because that would take the guts out of the whole thing.'" After that, the initiative appeared to go nowhere. And when the top official stepped down from her post, it was all over. "People need to get over being afraid to come out and say boys are different. That's not a bad thing, and it's the only way to further the debate. If you try to wishy-washy your way through we're going nowhere."

School bureaucrats are terrified that advocating for boys will bring the charge they're ignoring girls, said Scieszka. "They need to start thinking of this the same way we went about doing something for girls with math and science. We just recognized that girls need to learn math and science in a different way. Why wouldn't we do the same for boys?" Scieszka asks exactly the right question. But doing that involves far more than just supplying teachers with boy-friendly books. It requires acknowledging that boys—and often, just boys alone—need extra tools to help them cope with the early literacy demands being thrust upon them.

In researching this book I came across no evidence, here in the United States or abroad, that reaching out to improve boys' school performance sets back girls. In school districts that have experimented with large-scale efforts to help boys, such as the upper-middle-class Edina district in suburban Minneapolis, the boys benefited from the interventions—and so did the girls. Objecting to helping boys out of fear of hurting girls makes a good ideological sound bite but lacks any credibility when it comes to the realities of the classroom.

VOLUNTEER FOR RESEARCH-BASED
TUTORING PROGRAMS

One day as I was sifting through the day's mail I found an appeal for reading tutors at an elementary school a few miles from my home in Arlington, Virginia. With a little training you can become a "book buddy" for a struggling reader, the ad said. Given that the premise of my book was that boys weren't being taught to read, the idea of "walking the walk" seemed reasonable, and soon I found myself at an elementary school serving Latino and African-American parents and students living in a neglected neighborhood sandwiched between major highways and the Arlington National Cemetery.

My charge was a good-natured, African-American second grader who tolerated my early fumbling while trying to master a well-designed tutoring program developed by University of Virginia reading experts. His regular teacher pinpointed his reading weaknesses for the full-time Book Buddy coordinator, who then translated the teacher's advice into a scripted instruction program that changed with each session. My job was to follow the script and make it interesting.

Spinning through the multiple, fast-moving drills designed to teach an eight-year-old how to sort out the long A's from the short A's proved to be as valuable for my book research as it was for him. It didn't take long to figure out how much work was involved with teaching reading and how easy it would be for any elementary teacher swamped with a class of twenty-five kids, each of whom is working at different levels, to look the other way as he slipped through the cracks. While this boy was lucky enough to have parents and teachers determined to avoid that, thousands of boys like him are simply promoted through the grades without any sense of the long A's, short A's, or scores of other critical reading skills.

In years past, boys always seemed to recover from their literacy deficiencies. But the world has changed around them. Now, allowing these boys to pass through elementary school as struggling readers amounts to condemning them to an underclass life. Winning help for struggling readers, however, won't be as easy as it sounds. Elementary school educators either swamped with other duties or mindful of the don't-worry-about-the-boys mantra from skeptics don't always act. That's where community volunteers come in.

What struck me about the Book Buddies program was its precision. The tutor just piggybacks on scientific heavy lifting already carried out by the Ph.D.s at the University of Virginia. It made me feel like a pro. Book Buddies is not the only highly targeted tutoring program I came across. At Frankford Elementary in Delaware, a school of mostly poor children whose rankings went from last to first in the county, principal Duncan Smith credits the school tutoring programs for having a "major impact" on student achievement. When I visited Frankford, the school drew on 160 volunteer tutors to work with more than 120 students. My suggestion: If your local school lacks a program such as Book Buddies, lobby the principal to start one. These programs make obsolete the near-worthless hand-holding volunteer programs many schools offer up.

INTENSIFY LITERACY INSTRUCTION IN MIDDLE AND HIGH SCHOOL

After the elementary grades, most schools make a gradual transition from literacy skills to literature skills, leaving behind thousands of weak readers, most of them boys. Current federal reading programs, such as Striving Readers, are aimed at kindergarten through third grade. In most schools, that means the faltering readers in middle and high school receive nothing beyond the usual classroom instruction that has failed to reach them in the past. Why not extend that program to the upper grades?, ask politicians such as Sen. Jeff Sessions (R-Ala.), who is married to a former teacher. Sessions raises the right question.

High schools that push hard on literacy usually see a payoff. Anyone walking into Alabama's Montevallo High School sees that something different is going on. Student work ranging from poetry to regular writing assignments lines "word walls." Montevallo, located about forty miles southwest of Birmingham, joined the Alabama Reading Initiative in 2002, which guided the school in making literacy the subject of every class. "We've always been a good little school, but at the high school level it's easy to splinter off," the principal told me. "It's easy for the social studies teachers to just care about social studies and the math teachers to just care about math."[5]

What started as a faculty book club exercise grew into a collaborative effort to turn every teacher into a reading teacher. Said the reading coach, "You will not hear a math teacher or a science teacher at this school say, 'I'm not a reading teacher.' They know how to teach reading."

MAKE HIGH SCHOOL MORE RELEVANT

The California probes into the growing gender imbalances in state colleges and universities there didn't have to look far to find the problem: Boys could care less about high school. Their grades were poor, their course work was weak, and their test scores low. As a result, 58 percent of the students who qualified for admission to the University of California campuses were girls. Giving boys a reason to care about high school is a problem that has been solved, at least in part. Here are two examples:

High Tech High

Larry Rosenstock has a simple explanation for why his California High Tech High Schools have been outstanding successes, especially among boys. They combine head and hand, which is what he did after leaving the law to teach carpentry. "I was teaching carpentry to working-class boys who were every bit as bright as the middle-class guys I was in law school with, but they didn't think of themselves that way . . . a lot of boys get shunted into programs that misassume what they can and can't do, and a lot of those assumptions are based on class."

Rosenstock's carpentry students thrived under the physical and intellectual demands placed on them. Now, with backing from California high-tech money including the Gates Foundation and Qualcomm executive Gary Jacobs, Rosenstock has fashioned eight hands-on learning schools that combine the best of old-style vocational education with the best of a college-prep curriculum that includes high-level literacy skills. The schools are swamped with applications from both teachers and students, 60 percent of whom are boys. Many of those boys are nonwhite and come from low-income families.

Boys in the large comprehensive high schools in California and elsewhere in the country often don't see the purpose of learning. At High Tech High, students get their hands on state-of-the-art tech gear no matter what subject they're studying.

"We play to a broader range of modalities that capture boys in ways other schools don't." Both girls and boys thrive at High Tech High, said Rosenstock. "We hire a lot of young women with Ph.D.s in math and science and the girls see this and think, 'This could be me.'"

Rosenstock's schools avoid the sit-in-your-seat lectures that girls endure better than boys. "Boys are just not wired that way. They're more kinesthetic. They need to bounce off the walls." Hundreds of visitors come to the High Tech Highs to witness the programs there, said Rosenstock. At the end of the tour, he always asks the same question: What surprised you the most? And he always gets the same answer: "We've never seen such a high percentage of kids engaged in active learning."

Career Academies

At the nearly new Braden River High School in Bradenton, Florida, students choose one of four career-path study areas: engineering/leadership, arts/communication, science/health, and business/international studies. All the coursework within those academies slips neatly into those themes. "If you are taking a medical class and acquiring a new vocabulary, in English class you will learn how to spell that vocabulary, know the definition, and write a report on that health issue. It makes that English class valuable to them," said Angie Grasberger, who coordinates the career academy programs in Manatee County schools.

The assumption that this is a gambit to keep poor and minority students coming to school and focused on the coursework would be wrong. Braden River High School serves nearly all white, upper-middle-class students, nearly all of whom plan to go on to college. Braden River is a "choice" high school in Manatee County, which means those upper-class parents and students deliberately chose a career academy education. This is not even remotely connected to the "voc-ed" of thirty years ago.

"I was a math teacher," said Grasberger, "and I could teach any student how to solve an algebraic equation. But if you want to go into medicine you'll need to know how to use that equation. As a nurse, calculating dosages of medication depends on whether you're dealing with an adult or child. That's algebra. Kids in career academies see the relationships between skills they need and the academics in the classroom."

Valerie Jones, assistant principal at Braden River High, says her school offers the same college-prep curriculum as other schools, including seventeen advanced placement courses. "But in addition we give them a career-themed curriculum." The engineering/leadership academy has a special appeal to boys, who make up nearly 80 percent of its classes. "If it's appealing to the students they will want to come to class," said Jones. The traditional English classes, where students march through the usual high school "classics," have been replaced. "How do they give these students any real-world experience?" asks Jones. In English class, students in the business academy might research and write papers on how successful companies were formed.

There are more than three hundred career academies around the country, and they appear to be succeeding, according to researchers from Manpower Demonstration Research Corp., who studied ten academies in several states. They attract a diverse student body, encourage teachers to get to know students better, and reduce dropout rates, according to the study.[6]

TEACH BOYS AND GIRLS SEPARATELY? (MAYBE)

The suggestion that boys and girls learn both differently and at different paces is not a controversial notion, at least to parents. I recall volunteering in my daughter's first grade class and watching as the children were assigned the task of writing out letters. Holding their pencils properly, the girls carefully sketched out looping, flowing letters in near-perfect fashion. The boys, meanwhile, gripped their pencils like exotic daggers and succeeded mostly at tearing holes in the paper. Wow, I thought, imagine the odds of my daughter landing in a class full of boys bound for special education pullouts. Did I ever have a lot to learn. A few years later some of those same boys so inept at tracing letters were packed off to the district's gifted and talented schools, well on their trajectories to MIT and Caltech.

So, if boys and girls truly do learn differently, why are there so few options, short of private schools, for parents to educate their sons and daughters in same-sex classrooms or schools? Perhaps *that* could explain why boys are falling so far behind. In 2006 the advocates of single-sex education got their wish when the federal Education Department opened up a legal path for public schools to experiment with single-sex education. The pent-up demand was evident: Within two years, 514 schools around the country offered that option to parents. In a typical school, a principal with four first grade classes would offer two of the four as single-sex options. Most principals discovered an enthusiastic response from parents, resulting in wait lists of children wanting into the single-sex class.

The single-sex option fell on especially fertile ground in South Carolina, which by 2008 had nearly two hundred schools offering single-sex options and another two hundred lined up to join the experiment. In Greenville, South Carolina, principal Vaughan Overman couldn't be more pleased with the single-sex teaching experiment she launched in 2008 at Taylors Elementary. Teachers embraced it. Parents loved it. One immediate payoff was a plunge in the number of discipline referrals. At Taylors, teachers leaned heavily on Dr. Leonard Sax's book *Why Gender Matters*. Sax, a pediatrician who founded the National Association for the Advancement of Single Sex Public Schools, offers educators the specifics of learning differences, everything from how loud or soft a teacher should speak (girls like it softer) to the classroom temperature (boys like it about six degrees cooler). Some of Sax's other learning differences include:

- *Girls' hearing is far more sensitive.* Eleven-year-old girls are distracted by noise levels about ten times softer than noise levels that boys find distracting. "That boy who's tap-tap-tapping his fingers on the desk might not be bothering the other boys, but he is bothering the girls—as well as the (female) teacher."

- *Boys and girls develop skills at different times.* "In girls, the language areas of the brain develop before the areas used for spatial relations and for geometry. In boys, it's the other way around."

- *Connections to emotions differ.* "In girls, emotion is processed in the same area of the brain that processes language. So, it's easy for most girls to talk about their emotions." Just the opposite holds true for boys. "The hardest question for many boys to answer is: 'Tell me how you feel.'" The exact question they get asked to answer in book reports.

For Sax, the obvious conclusion from the brain differences is that some boys and girls benefit from single-sex classrooms. His logic is appealing. Pushing reading skills too fast for boys, for example, risks turning them off to reading. Hence, you find boys in sixth grade who barely read anything beyond the instruction manuals for video games. The same holds true for girls and math. Teaching boys and girls the same material at the same pace has backfired, writes Sax. "Gender gaps in some areas have widened in the past three decades. The proportion of girls studying subjects such as physics and computer science has dropped in half. Boys are less likely to study subjects such as foreign languages, history, and music than they were three decades ago. The ironic result of three decades of gender blindness has been an intensifying of gender stereotypes."

Enter a classroom at Taylors and you'll see the Sax theories in action. The all-girls classes are bathed in full-power lights with the desks arranged in social style, facing one another. The girls usually have their own cubby somewhere in the class. Academic exercises are conducted collaboratively with the girls working in groups. In the all-boys classes, the lights are dimmer, in some cases coming from floor lamps. The desks are arranged side-by-side to avoid direct confrontations, and academic exercises at times resemble athletic events with lots of manipulatives and moving around.

All this sounds great, and it may work. The problem is, nobody knows. The Bush administration viewed the single-sex experiment in the same light as it did Wall Street: deregulate and allow free enterprise to sort everything out. When the department issued its go-ahead decision, schools were offered no research on how to conduct the experiment. As a result, schools eager to try it—in most cases prompted by the boy troubles—were left on their own. Odder yet, the department didn't launch any research to track what was playing out in the 514 schools experimenting with single-sex education by the end of 2008. That left educators to be guided by single-sex advocates such as Sax and Michael Gurian, author of books such as *Boys and Girls Learn Differently*. Here's a quick look at Gurian's philosophy, which leans heavily on breakthroughs in brain imaging. Writes Gurian, "New positron emission tomography (PET) and MRI [magnetic resonance imaging] technologies enable us to look inside the brains of boys and girls, where we find structural and functional differences that profoundly affect human learning." Those differences, say Gurian, include:

- Girls' superior writing skills may arise from their stronger neural connectors, which give them more detailed memory storage, superior listening skills, and better discrimination among voice tones.

- Boys' superior abilities to move objects around in their head probably results from boys having more cortical areas dedicated to spatial-mechanical functioning. By contrast, boys use about half the brain space that girls use for verbal-emotive functions.

- Girls are less impulsive than boys because their prefrontal cortex is more active than boys' and matures at earlier ages. Higher serotonin levels in the bloodstream and brains also make girls less impulsive.

- Boys tend to drift off in class because their brain "is set to renew, recharge, and reorient itself by entering what neurologists call a rest state."

Biological differences account for the superior verbal abilities of girls, writes Gurian. "The female brain tends to drive itself toward stimulants, like reading and writing that involve complex texture, tonality, and mental activity."

Biological differences also lend credence to the stereotypes about boys being better at math, according to Gurian. "These typical 'boy' qualities in the brain help illustrate why boys generally learn higher math and physics more easily than most girls do when those subjects are taught abstractly on the chalkboard; why more boys than girls play video games that involve physical movement . . . and why more boys than girls tend to get in trouble for impulsiveness."

Gurian and Sax could be right about all this, but there are a lot of nationally respected neuroscientists who say their ideas about brain-based learning differences are off target. Lise Eliot, associate professor of neuroscience at the Chicago Medical School of Rosalind Franklin University, wrote this for *USA Today:*

> While subtle gender differences exist in sensory, motor, cognitive and emotional skills, sex typically accounts for only 1% to 5% of the total variance—meaning the range of such abilities is much larger within a group of girls or boys than between the sexes. And yet, we have educators who believe they should separate boys and girls because of differences in hearing or visual abilities, serotonin or oxytocin levels, corpus callosum or planum temporale sizes.
>
> Sex differences are sexy. Scientists often publish data showing profound gender similarities, but these studies rarely make it into public view. Rather, it is the studies reporting gender differences, however small or tentative, that are hyped. The same is true for research on single-sex K–12 education, which has generally found that success in such settings is not caused by gender segregation per se, or even gender-geared instructional techniques, but to the high expectations, dedicated faculty, family involvement and engaged students who choose to attend such schools.

I lack the qualifications to weigh in on the neuroscience argument. But my reporting tells me there are good reasons to doubt that the surge in experiments with single-sex education will make a significant difference for boys. Hundreds of public schools have launched single-sex experiments, mostly out of despair over lagging boys. But most of those schools were launched before they had a good sense of what actually works in single-sex education. For that, I fault the U.S. Department of Education. I'm not suggesting that single-sex schools lack merit—our two daughters graduated from girls schools. In the spring of 2009 a British researcher released the results of a large-scale study of students in single-sex classes, finding boys do better in English when there are no girls in the class and girls do better in single-sex math and science classes.[7] I have no reason to doubt the merit of single-sex education. I just fear the rushed experiment in the United States will backfire. In fact, we may be seeing signs of that happening. In August 2009, the school board in Williamsburg, S.C., killed off a single-sex experiment there. Board vice-chair Norma Bartelle said she didn't like what she saw in single-sex classes: "The boys would answer questions when they were thrown a football," she said, "[w]hile the girls would answer by sitting face to face." Bartelle complained that such methods enforced the idea that boys like sports and girls enjoy conversing and gossiping.[8] If schools don't see immediate payoffs, the experiments will be abandoned, perhaps prematurely.

REVAMP COMMUNITY COLLEGES

Jim Catanzaro, president of Chattanooga State Technical Community College, found himself watching over an unsettling trend of a campus skewing female. In only one decade, between 1996 and 2006, the campus shifted from half female to 62 percent female. Chattanooga is not alone among community colleges, where the gender gaps exceed those at four-year colleges. By the year 2000, women were earning 151 associate's degrees for every 100 earned by men.[9]

Where did the men go? Catanzaro and other college officials spent two years trying to answer that question. The causes they identified included a booming construction and tourism industry, military recruitment, and high schools that weren't interesting to boys—in the slightest. In sampling high school boys, Catanzaro determined that what really mattered to high school boys were cars, especially racing. Catanzaro concluded that going with the flow was smarter than fighting it, so in 2006 the college launched an institute for building and construction. The idea was to target tradesmen looking to move up as project managers or entrepreneurs. Almost instantly, the program drew a hundred new students, all male. Next came a motor sports program, which was really a new engineering program in disguise. "It's an umbrella," said Catanzaro. "Students who come in become engineering technology majors, but all the lab work they do will be on cars, boats, or motorcycles, all related to racing. If they're studying metallurgy it's as it relates to the high end of racing. Same thing with hydraulics."

That program produced a similar surge of male students. In just one year, the gender imbalances reversed course for the first time in a decade. What puzzles Catanzaro is why so few community colleges have not restructured their course offerings in similar ways. "I've talked to other community college presidents about it and their eyes glaze over. They say it doesn't seem to be a real problem. But these gender imbalance numbers just fly right in your face. I don't get it."

Catanzaro's question is a good one. Perhaps the community colleges are satisfied with the surge in growth they've enjoyed from women signing on for training in growing health care fields. While a few community colleges have adjusted their marketing to appeal to boys, colleges rarely realign their courses to appeal to males, he said. Just changing marketing strategies, however, is not enough. "These [gender trends] are powerful forces. I concluded early on that marketing alone wasn't going to do it," said Catanzaro. "You have to go to where the men are."

Possibly the most interesting community college story in America is found in Maine, a state with a university system with some of the widest gender gaps in the nation. In late 2006, when I saw a magazine article saying that Maine's community college enrollment had jumped 48 percent in only four years, I contacted community college officials, expecting to be told about looming gender gaps. Just the opposite. Over the past sev-

eral years the percentage of male students in that system has been growing. In recent years, more men than women enrolled.

How can this be, I asked Maine Community College System president
John Fitzsimmons? As it turned out, I had asked Fitzsimmons one of his
favorite questions. Several years ago Fitzsimmons and other community
college officials took a hard look at Maine's high school population and
saw something others had missed. "It was surprising how many students
were academically capable of going to college but weren't. These were
students right on the edge who could go either way. What we found most
of the time with the vast majority of these kids is they would be the first
in the family to go to college. Plus, they had no savings put aside and
found the whole process daunting, particularly the financial process."

Most of these were C-average students—students Fitzsimmons dubs
"drop in" students. They went to high school because it was required, not
because they were in love with learning. "These were the kids who sat in
the middle of the class, never caused anyone trouble, and would do
enough to pass but weren't academically fired up about it." Most of these
drop-in students never considered a four-year degree that might or might
not lead to a good-paying job. With these students in mind Fitzsimmons
created the Early College for ME program. Begun in 2003, the program
works to help these students get ready academically and offers scholarships
to cover half a year's tuition at one of the state's seven community colleges. As explained in Chapter 7, boys in Maine need the extra help.

Many of the students were shocked when they were told "I think you
can do college," said Fitzsimmons. "The students really blossomed under
this program." Most striking was the number of boys who signed up.
These boys could see job training potential in community college they
couldn't see in four-year colleges, said Fitzsimmons. Among the young
men entering through this program, 83 percent preselected a profession
to study, ranging from computers to culinary arts. "The idea of putting
life into shorter bites appears to fit well with these guys," said Fitzsimmons, "whereas four years sounds like a long time and a lot of debt."

KEEP GIVING GUYS BREAKS IN COLLEGE ADMISSIONS . . . FOR JUST A LITTLE LONGER

In June 2007, writer Alex Kingsbury of *U.S. News & World Report* embarrassed college admissions offices around the country with an investigation into admissions biases against girls—attempts to keep campus gender gaps in check by reaching deeper into the application pool to choose less qualified boys.[10] Virginia's University of Richmond, for example, admits women at a rate thirteen percentage points lower than the admittance rate for men, and even that's not enough to keep the student population at an even 50–50 balance. The University of Richmond is private, which protects it somewhat from legal challenges to the admissions bias. Far less protected, however, is the College of William & Mary, another Virginia college featured in the article. William & Mary is a public college that admits women at a rate twelve percentage points lower than the male rate.

The University of Richmond and the College of William & Mary are among scores, perhaps hundreds, of colleges quietly engaged in admissions discrimination designed to keep campus gender imbalances in check. While the boy troubles lie at the heart of why colleges have to offer admissions preferences to young men, an important question to answer is: How do the colleges get away with such blatant discrimination? The short answer is, because just about everyone wants them to get away with it. Parents of lagging boys appreciate the boost. Co-eds want to attend a gender-balanced college. Even feminist leaders avert their eyes—in the name of diversity.

I think they're right; the preferences need to continue. My daughters disagree with me on this one. Several years ago when they graduated from high school and entered the chilling competition to win a seat at a selective college, they were well aware that their grades, extracurriculars, and test scores had to exceed that of boys vying for the same spots in that freshman class. And they weren't happy about it. When I wrote an editorial for *USA Today* advocating admissions breaks for boys, they volunteered to write our "opposing view" explaining how wrong I was.

In fact, many boy advocates agree with my daughters. Granting preferences to boys, dubbed gender weighting, only masks the problem, say gender experts such as Tom Mortenson. I grant Mortenson's point, but I also defend a college's academic right to choose the freshman class of its preference. If a college wants more violinists, rugby players, African Americans . . . or men, that should be its academic freedom to choose. And preserving that academic freedom grants a little breathing space for boys who have been turned off by high school. Fixing that problem could take decades. Besides, there are creative ways to admit boys without employing the heavy thumb of gender weighting.

One option arose in 2006 out of Baltimore's Towson University, which created a new recruiting category: low grades/high scores. Even though the program is not limited to boys, that pretty much describes thousands of high school boys around the country. Even if boys start thriving in academics their junior or senior years, their near-collapse in ninth grade guarantees them less-than-stellar grade-point averages. And yet their tests scores usually look pretty good, especially on the SAT college admissions test, which leans toward the aptitude side of learning measurement.

At Towson, students who earned no better than a 2.8 high school grade-point average, which is too low for Towson, got a hard look if their SAT scores were in the 1200 or higher range.[11] "That cohort has a fairly high percentage of males in it," said Towson president Robert Caret. "Those of you who are parents of boys might know what I'm talking about."[12] What Towson did is exactly what James Madison University debated doing but backed away from. There are two reasons why JMU and others will hesitate in following Towson on a boy-friendly admissions path. First, universities such as JMU that are heavily female have found success in catering to women, which creates a don't-mess-with-the-customer wariness. Second, the universities are all too aware of the hypocrisy that such a policy would create. As a parent who has been through the college search twice in recent years, I've heard this bromide multiple times: What we really look for is proof of effort, which comes from high grades earned in tough courses, say the college admissions officers in their group meetings with parents. As for test scores, those are tertiary.

Another tricky downside to the Towson approach is the solid research showing that grades, not test scores, predict how a student will do in college. In other words, smart boys who slacked their way through high school have an unsettling way of doing that all over again in college. For lack of a better description, let's call it the Beavis and Butt-head factor, a factor Towson seems all too aware of. Young men entering Towson through that funnel sign a contract agreeing to meet regularly with an academic adviser, attend twice weekly study halls, and earn at least a 2.0 average in their freshman year. Only after those hurdles are cleared is the student considered a bona fide Towson student.[13]

The men entering Towson appear oblivious to any stigma involved. "It sort of sounds like affirmative action for boys, if you will," said freshman Chris Beck, who entered with a C-plus average and 1240 SAT scores. "But it doesn't bother me."[14] Towson officials are quick to point out that this program is not just for men, but well over 80 percent of the students in the program (forty admitted the first year, seventy-four the next year) are men. So far, the program has been a mixed success, the associate provost at Towson told me. The program suffers a steep attrition rate, she said, in part because the recruits fail to follow rules such as mandatory study hall appearances. "Some think they don't have to follow the rules, and life isn't like that."

What Towson learned in the pilot program—which was eliminated in 2007—was that good test takers aren't necessarily good students. "The SAT is not as good a predictor of how you'll do in college as the high school GPA," said the Towson official. Yes, and that's exactly why women are ruling the academic world. Grades trump test scores. The Towson formula may have to be tweaked . . . but regardless of dissent from my daughters, I'm sticking with it: Boys need breaks, at least for now.

EXPERIMENT MORE WITH K–12 READING PROGRAMS

Lisby Elementary, Aberdeen, Maryland

Ten-year-old Frank is precisely the kind of boy Maryland state education superintendent Nancy Grasmick had in mind when she risked ridicule in 2004 by launching a comic book curriculum experiment in elementary school.[15] If you think assigning kids reading that involves the antics of Donald Duck and Uncle Scrooge sounds bizarre, well, you have a point. And yet that's what Maryland began experimenting with two years ago after taking a sober look at how far behind boys were in reading. "You see kids reading comic books, buying comic books and they seem totally engrossed," said Grasmick. "It looks like there's some potential there."[16]

That would describe Frank, a polite and formal sort of boy whose face lights up when asked the height of the stack of comic books he has stashed away in his bedroom. "This high?" I ask, raising my hand a foot off the table where he is eating his lunch at George Lisby Elementary School, located in a threadbare neighborhood of Aberdeen, Maryland, near the Delaware border. Frank smiles and shakes his head no. "This high?" I ask again, raising my hand to two feet off the table. Yes, that high, he acknowledges with pride. Born to a family of émigrés from Cameroon, this is Frank's third elementary school. He started out in an elementary school in New York City, and then entered an elementary school in inner-city Baltimore. This is his first year at Lisby, but he can't believe his good fortune: Comic books handed out in school!

Before you turn up your nose in revulsion, consider that Frank has more than comic books in his bedroom. He read the most recent Harry Potter book and he makes his way to the local library every week to pick up traditional chapter books. Frank's favorite chapter books are those where you get to select how the adventure turns out. Encouraging reluctant readers, especially boys, to turn the corner from comic books (and from there to the more sophisticated graphic novels and from there to traditional literature) is what the Maryland program has in mind. "We do surveys of our adult corrections population and when you look at the reading levels they're often at the fourth grade level. I see what happens when you have reluctant readers,"[17] said Grasmick. (Although studies cannot predict the size of prison populations based on reading levels in elementary schools, state authorities remain intrigued by the startling low literacy levels found among prisoners.)

To design a program targeting those reluctant readers, Grasmick assembled a team of reading specialists who tackled the problem using reverse engineering. Interviews with successful boy readers revealed they often became hooked on comic books early and then transferred that interest to broader literature by sixth grade. Frank's fifth grade teacher, Ronald Wooden, has happily wrapped comic books and graphic novels into his teachings. "I perceive of them as any other piece of literature. They have story lines, characters, just like you'd find in another piece of literature."

One difference, said Wooden, is that boys tend to grasp them. "Boys' brains are very spatial, very competitive, and when you look at comic books you see lots of action." Prior to adopting this new curriculum, a typical book offered at Lisby was *Bridge to Terabithia*,[18] a boy/girl fantasy story. "The boys could have cared less." When Wooden reviews the books pegged to the ages of his students, he sees an imbalance. "A lot of these novels are focused to girls, not all of them, but a majority out there. A lot of love stories, which the girls want to read." Comic books, he says, help level that gap by giving boys plots chock full of superhero-driven action.

On the day I visited Lisby, Wooden conducted a whole-class session using a Donald Duck comic book, pressing the students to analyze the text and pictures for mood, tone, and character development. It seemed odd, melding a sophisticated literature analysis discussion to a story about Donald Duck scrambling to avoid being eaten by dinosaurs or shot up by robots. Then Wooden separated the boys and girls and conducted an all-boys session to discuss the thick graphic novel "Bones," a book that in appearance is akin to something you'd see a Japanese boy reading on a bullet train.

What struck me in both cases was how natural both the boy and girl students found it, especially the boys. I rarely see boys that excited about breaking down a novel into its working parts—not something that usually intrigues them. In May 2007, Grasmick announced that the comic book/graphic novel experiment in eight elementary schools was successful enough to warrant expansion into some middle schools. The state worked with Disney Publishing Worldwide and Diamond Comic Distributors to develop kits for two hundred classrooms. "We never said this program would supplant . . . our regular reading program," said Grasmick, "but it could provide a huge motivation for some of our students."[19]

The Comic Book Project, run out of Columbia University, is now in 860 schools around the country. "It's very much a teacher-led kind of movement in that teachers are looking for ways to engage their children, and they're finding some of that in comic books," its director told me. "For kids who may be struggling and for kids who may be new to the English language, that visual sequence is a very powerful tool."[20]

HELP MEN ALREADY AT COLLEGES

Lakeland Community College in the eastern suburbs of Cleveland is one of hundreds of community colleges faced with gender problems they can't solve. Fewer men enroll. More men who do enroll have academic problems, and far more women than men end up graduating. Worst of all, things just keep getting worse. In 1996 Lakeland hired Jim Shelley to run its Men's Resource Center, a rarity at any two- or four-year college. When Shelley looked at the gender breakdowns there, he found that men were 58 percent more likely to be put on academic notice and 40 percent more likely to be dismissed. The grade-point average for men was 2.64, compared to 2.85 for women. And despite those academic problems, men were a third less likely to use the college's tutorial services.[21]

One promising project Shelley oversees is Gateway to College, which reaches out to men who never considered themselves college material. "We put them into a one-credit-hour class for free, which gives them an opportunity to test drive a college class. Most of these guys are a couple of years out of high school and upon leaving said 'no more teachers, no more books,' but now find themselves in a situation where they have to pursue an education and are pretty apprehensive about doing so."

Many men leave high school for what they see as high-paying jobs on manufacturing lines, utility poles, or in mines, only to discover a few years later that their jobs have been outsourced or their bodies just aren't up to the stress, stamina, and risk that brought them the high wages in the first place. "The biggest thing I run up against is how you get these guys to come back to school when they've become breadwinners for their families." The answer, says Shelley, is to send retooled workers into high schools to tell men the risk they take in avoiding college.

At Florida's St. Petersburg College, Rod Davis oversees the Male Outreach Initiative. "Our president caught wind of what's going on nationally and has decided to allocate funds to be proactive at getting a program for men here." The first task Davis undertook was studying what other colleges were doing for men. It didn't take long to discover that not much was happening. "It really shows there's neglect with this issue. Other colleges I've talked to would say, 'Hey, it's great you guys are actually the lead on this.'"

Davis found it odd that colleges were neglecting the issue. At St. Petersburg, the percentage of men has dropped to 37 percent, which is below the national average. "But if you look at this as a trend it's going to get low like this everywhere." If colleges run recruitment/retention programs for men, they tend to focus solely on minority males. Although only 16 percent of St. Petersburg's student population is minority, Davis was able to draw on lessons from programs such as the Black Male Initiative at the City University of New York. "It doesn't really matter if you're Hispanic, African-American, or white. Men are looking for the same thing. They are looking to come to school, get a job, and eventually get a career. It's the 'in between' they don't know."

Davis will also draw from a St. Petersburg program that channels help to women called Women on the Way, which has operated on campus for more than twenty years. But he knows working with men will be more challenging. "Guys won't ask for help. We're dealing with a difficult customer base." The irony of running a women's help group for more than twenty years while male enrollment has slid to 37 percent is not lost on Davis.[22] At least his college is doing something, he points out.

COLLECT THE NUMBERS ON BOYS! (AND USE THE NUMBERS FOR SCHOOL ACCOUNTABILITY)

There's an odd aversion to collecting data along gender lines. Race, ethnicity, age, income—all okay. But gender, not so much. In the national tests, such as college admissions SAT and ACT, gender breakouts are available. And they are available in the federal sampling test, the National Assessment of Educational Progress.

Where gender data is often missing is at the local and state level. Most egregious are the national education advocacy groups, the well-funded research/think tank groups that issue reports on everything from college readiness to third grade reading proficiency. When I phone for the gender breakdowns in their studies I can nearly always predict the answer: We only did it for race. But is race enough? In Chicago, boys and girls from the same families, the same schools, and the same neighborhoods are turning out radically different, a phenomenon Chicago schools researcher Melissa Roderick has dubbed the "genderization of race." (There's nothing unique about boys and girls in Chicago. It's just that they bothered to break their numbers out by gender.)

Most school districts remain oblivious to the issue, mostly because nobody requires them to pay attention. While most teachers and parents will tell you that state and federal school accountability has overreached, in the case of gender it has underreached. Merely adding gender to the state and federal (No Child Left Behind) formula that determines where a school lands on the "needs improvement" list would produce some lively discussions in local schools, where mothers would demand answers for why their local school allows their sons to fall behind. In the end, schools most likely would discover a positive: Targeting boys is a promising strategy for keeping the entire school off "needs improvement" accountability lists.

STRIKE A DEAL WITH NATIONAL FEMINIST LEADERS

Frankly, I have a hard time deciding which is more ludicrous, the suggestion that feminists are responsible for the gender gaps or that boy advocates are part of a vast conspiracy to roll back gains for women. As discussed earlier, the feminists' hands are clean of responsibility for boys falling behind. And as the father of two daughters I'd be quick to detect whether boy advocates are part of a backlash movement against women. Every cause has some odd outliers, but overall I just don't see it.

Higher education expert Tom Mortenson, who has become a passionate advocate for boys, despairs of being called antifeminist. "I try to phrase this as a woman's issue as much as a man's issue," said Mortenson. "There are a lot of gorgeous, well-educated single women out there who simply can't find a man to partner with. They're twenty-five or thirty years old and they don't have a serious boyfriend. They always thought the men would be there, but they're not. It's very painful. . . . At some point I really think the feminists are going to come around to the point of view that they have as much stake in this as the men." I suspect Mortenson is right. Eventually, the pushback movement will discover they're fighting a battle that doesn't need to be fought.

Leaders such as Kim Gandy, the longtime president of NOW, have everything to gain and nothing to lose by acknowledging the obvious: that boys are in trouble. Reaching out to help young men will in the long run help women as well. Anyone who doubts that needs to sit down and have a chat with Oprah about the damage the looming gender gaps have inflicted on the African-American community. If national feminist groups change their position, so will the two national teachers unions.

Once a truce is declared, educators can take a fresh look at why so many boys arrive in twelfth grade unprepared for college work and why so many young men who do go to college drop out before earning degrees. Is it really because classrooms are feminized? Is it really because their minds were warped by video games? Is it really because mothers cut the apron strings prematurely? Based on what I've learned in my travels, careful researchers won't settle on any of those as the primary causes for these academic lapses. Nor will they find the problem is limited only to poor and minority boys. A one-day tour of Chicago and its suburbs will settle that debate quickly. At this point, readers are familiar with my central argument: The world has gotten more verbal; boys haven't. The point of writing the book, however, is less to convince the world I'm "right" than to persuade the U.S. Department of Education to start the long-delayed task of laying out the causes and solutions for the gender gaps. If the Aussies and Brits can do it, why can't we?

The Facts About Boys

1. *School Grades.* The grade advantage long held by girls appears to be broadening. In 1990, both girls and boys had C-average grade-point averages (2.77 for girls, 2.59 for boys), according to the High School Transcripts Study (U.S. Department of Education). By 2005 the gap widened to a B-average for girls (3.09) and a C-plus for boys (2.86).

   The 2007 survey of college freshmen conducted by the Higher Education Research Institute shows 28 percent of women reporting a high school grade-point average of A or A+, compared to 21 percent of men.

   The pattern appears to hold in school districts serving high-income students. In the Wilmette School District in Illinois, which serves the neighborhoods around Northwestern University, 75 percent of the fifth grade girls earned an A in reading, compared to 54 percent of the boys. In math, 70 percent of the fifth grade girls earned an A, compared to 54 percent of the boys.

2. *Top Academic Honors.* Twice as many girls as boys were members of the National Honor Society in 2007. In recent years

as more high schools adopted policies of honoring all A-average students as valedictorians, it has become routine to read newspaper stories about clusters of all-female valedictorians. Girls hold their own on prestigious science awards: From 2006 through 2008, all the first place winners of the Intel Science Search were female. From 2001 through 2008, five females and three males took top place.

The conventional wisdom about boys and girls—that girls excel in reading and writing while boys dominate in math and science—is being upended. In June 2009, the journal *Science* published a study showing that on average, boys do no better than girls in math.[1] And at the high end of the scale—those with outstanding math skills—the gender gap that had long favored males was disappearing. On many state tests of math and science abilities, girls now outscore boys. While girls have closed the math/science gap, they continue to either maintain or increase the verbal abilities gap they enjoy over boys, according to several years of data from the federal National Assessment of Educational Progress.

3. *Grade Repetition, Special Education.* Nearly twice as many boys as girls repeat a grade. Among black males, more than one in ten repeats a grade. Among secondary students with disabilities, nearly 70 percent are male. Among students with emotional disabilities, 76 percent are male.

4. *Academic Diligence.* Fifty-four percent of female high school sophomores are enrolled in a college-preparatory curriculum, compared to 48 percent of males. Among female students, 43 percent have taken one to four advanced placement tests, compared to 39 percent of males.

5. *College Ambitions.* In 1980, federal surveys of high school seniors showed more boys than girls planning to earn four-year degrees. By 2001, those same surveys showed more than a ten-point gap favoring girls.

6. *Dropouts/Suspensions*. Estimates of dropout rates vary, but according to *Education Week* 32 percent of males drop out of school, compared to 25 percent of females. Among black males, 52 percent dropped out, compared to 39 percent of black females. In preschool, boys are four and a half times more likely to get expelled. In the K–12 years, boys are twice as likely to get suspended and three times as likely to get expelled.

7. *Higher Education*. Even though men and women reap identical benefits from earning postsecondary degrees (men outearn women, but the percentage increase from earning degrees is the same), a wide gender gap has opened up. Among whites, women earn 61 percent of associate degrees, 57 percent of bachelor's degrees, 62 percent of master's degrees, and 54 percent of doctoral degrees. Among blacks, women earn 61 percent of associate degrees, 66 percent of bachelor's degrees, 72 percent of master's degrees, and 64 percent of doctoral degrees.

   Often missed in the higher education numbers is the gender gap in "persistence" rates—the students who succeed in earning a degree within six years. That rate varies sharply depending on the university. Among highly selective colleges, graduation gender gaps are small but favor women. At state universities that draw nontraditional college students, the gender gaps can be sharp. At California State, Fullerton, for example, 55 percent of the women and 40 percent of the men graduate within six years. Nationally, when all kinds of colleges and universities are mixed together, the gender graduation gap shrinks. Depending on the study and the graduation time (graduation in four, five, or six years), the gender gap ranges from 6 percent to 10.4 percent, with women always ahead of the men.[2]

8. *Mental Health*. Among students ages 4 to 17, a fifth of parents have talked to a health care provider or school staff

member about their sons' emotional or behavioral problems, compared to just over a tenth of parents who did the same about their daughters' problems. Young boys (10 to 14) are twice as likely as young girls to commit suicide, and young men (20 to 24) are six times as likely. Although estimates vary, boys are roughly four times as likely to suffer from attention-deficit hyperactivity disorder.

9. *Racial Divides*. Saying that African-American and Hispanic males are faring poorly compared to whites doesn't get at the essential issue. What most people miss is that minority males are faring poorly compared to minority females. That's the "genderization" of race. Take writing: At the end of high school, 37 percent of black males fall into the "below basic" rating on federal assessments, compared to 17 percent of black females. A similar gender gap divides Hispanics. Over half of black males in twelfth grade score below basic in reading, compared to 40 percent of females. In 2004–2005, more than half of black males dropped out of high school, compared to 39 percent of black females.

10. *Literacy Skills*. At twelfth grade, more than a quarter of males rate as "below basic" writers on federal tests, compared to 11 percent of females. Just 16 percent of males at that age test as proficient/advanced writers, compared to 31 percent of females. In reading, a third of male students that age fall below basic, compared to 22 percent of females. Only 29 percent of male students are reading at the proficient/advanced levels, compared to 41 percent of females.

11. *"Disconnected" Youth*. Only recently have social scientists begun tracking the number of youths who are neither in school nor the workplace. Exact numbers are elusive, but researchers say twice as many males as females fall into this group. Those estimates are particularly striking for young

African-American males: 17 percent of black males age 16 to
24 are disconnected compared to 4 percent of white males,
according to Urban Institute researchers.

Primary source: *The State of American Boyhood.* Judith Kleinfeld, University of Alaska.
Springer Science & Business Media, 2009.

N O T E S

INTRODUCTION

1. Awards Assembly, May 18, 2006.

2. Bev McClendon and Annie Caulfield, phone interviews.

3. Stephanie Banchero and Darnell Little, "Girls Outpace Boys on Tests," *Chicago Tribune*, Oct. 31, 2007.

4. In the 2007 Monitoring the Future survey of seniors (University of Michigan), 53.9 percent of boys and 66.3 percent of girls said they would "definitely" graduate from a four-year college; 18.7 percent of boys and 25.7 percent of girls said they would "definitely" attend graduate or professional school after college.

5. E-mail correspondence with author.

6. Amy Crawford, "Gender Gap Widens for Colleges as Women Extend Lead," *Pittsburgh Tribune-Review*, Jan. 25, 2009.

7. Sandy Baum, economics professor and senior policy analyst for the College Board, personal conversations and data exchanges, and similar exchanges with several economists at the U.S. Department of Education. Regardless of the database used, male earnings are higher, but the percentage gain from earning a degree is almost identical for men and women. Best source: U.S. Department of Education's *Digest of Education Statistics,* median annual income of year-round, full-time workers 25 years old and over, by highest level of educational attainment and gender.

8. Michael Thompson, *Raising Cain* (New York: Ballantine, 1999).

9. Peg Tyre, "The Trouble with Boys," *Newsweek*, Jan. 30, 2006.

10. *Santa Fe Boys*, fall 2006.

CHAPTER 1: DISCOVERING THE PROBLEM

1. Interviews conducted on campus, December 2005.

2. Rick Barrett, "Paper-Industry Center Planned; College Will Share in Grant for Training," *Milwaukee Journal Sentinel*, Oct. 23, 2004.

3. Gale Holland, "California Faces Shortage of College Graduates for Workforce, Study Finds," *Los Angeles Times*, April 16, 2009.

4. Emily De Rocco, speech given on Oct. 28, 2004.

5. The sharpest gender gaps are found in urban schools. Chicago schools researcher Melissa Roderick decided to cut the data there not just by race and income but by gender as well. What she discovered was that boys and girls coming from the same homes, the same neighborhoods, and the same schools were turning out very differently. About half the boys graduating from Chicago public schools had less than a 2.0 average, compared to a fourth of the girls. Roderick then looked at graduation rates from the universities most of those college-bound Chicago students attended and found that students leaving high school with less than a 3.0 average were unlikely to complete college. Only 8 percent of the black males graduating from Chicago public schools had better than a 3.0, compared to 18 percent of the black girls. Roderick, a University of Chicago professor who is a veteran schools investigator with the Consortium on Chicago School Research, was struck by her findings. She coined a new term for it: the genderization of race. "From High School to the Future," Consortium on Chicago School Research, April 2006.

6. "How Schools Shortchange Girls," AAUW report, 1992.

7. Data from the 2004–2005 school years.

8. Matthew Pinzur and Stephanie Garry, "Most Dropouts Leave in Early High School," *Miami Herald,* June 21, 2006.

9. Jennifer Mrozowski, "DPS to Require Eighth Graders to Take Course for College Credit," *Detroit News*, Feb. 1, 2007.

CHAPTER 2: THE REASON FOR THE BOY TROUBLES

1. Eleanor Chute, "Never Too Early to Address Reading Problems," *Pittsburgh Post-Gazette*, Aug. 27, 2007.

2. Thomas Newkirk, *Misreading Masculinity: Boys, Literacy, and Popular Culture* (Portsmouth, NH: Heinemann, 2002).

3. Thomas Friedman, *The World Is Flat* (New York: Farrar, Straus and Giroux, 2005).

4. National Assessment of Educational Progress (National Center for Education Statistics).

5. Deborah Stipek and Sarah Miles, "Contemporaneous and Longitudinal Associations Between Social Behavior and Literacy Achievement in a Sample of Low-

Income Elementary School Children," *Child Development* 77, 1 (January/February 2006).

6. Jennifer Jordan, "State Worries Too Many Students Have Reading Problems" *Providence Journal*, Feb. 5, 2007.

7. http://www.eride.ri.gov/reportcard/06/rc2_state.asp?schcode = 00&grade = 11.

8. *Are Boys Making the Grade?* (Cambridge, MA: Rennie Center for Education Research & Policy, 2006).

9. "Analysis of WASL Scores Shows Boys Trailing Girls." *Seattle Times*, Dec. 4, 2005.

10. When the *Everett Herald* examined the gender gaps for 2006 it discovered that boys made up 66 percent of the students failing the writing test and 59 percent of the students failing the reading test. Melissa Slager and Eric Stevick, "Boys' WASL Scores Slow to Catch Up," *Everett* (Washington) *Herald*, March 11, 2007.

11. "Reading Between the Lines," www.act.org, Feb. 2006.

12. "Reading to Achieve: A Governor's Guide to Adolescent Literacy," www.nga.org, 2005.

13. "Reading at Risk," www.nasbe.org, Oct. 2005.

14. "Gender Gap in Reading," *Philadelphia Inquirer*, April 2, 2006.

15. Ibid.

16. Judith Kleinfeld, "Five Powerful Strategies for Connecting Boys to Schools," paper for White House conference, June 6, 2006. Reading data based on 2002 National Assessment of Educational Progress.

17. Sandra Stotsky, "The Influence of the K–12 Literature Curriculum on the Gender Gap and General Decline in Reading: What Research Suggests," paper presented to the 12th Conference of the Association of Literary Scholars and Critics, Oct. 13, 2006.

18. Gene Bottoms, phone interviews for editorial, "Boys' Academic Slide Calls for Accelerated Attention," *USA Today*, Dec. 22, 2003.

19. John Merrow, "First to Worst," PBS broadcast, Feb. 4, 2004.

CHAPTER 3: THE LIKELY CAUSES OF THE READING LAPSES

1. *Knowledge to Support the Teaching of Reading: Preparing Teachers for a Changing World*, eds. Catherine Snow, Peg Griffin, and M. Susan Burns (San Francisco: Jossey-Bass, 2005).

2. Kathleen Kennedy Manzo, "Books Calls for Radical Changes in Teacher Ed. to Improve Student Reading," *Education Week*, Dec. 23, 2005.

3. "What Education Schools Aren't Teaching About Reading and What Elementary Teachers Aren't Learning," National Council on Teacher Quality report, 2006.

4. The individual sounds that make up words. For example, "salt" has four phonemes, while "though" has only two phonemes. English has forty-one phonemes.

5. "Teacher Ed. Faulted on Reading Preparation," *Education Week*, June 7, 2006.

6. Arthur Levine, "Educating School Teachers," Education Schools Project report, Sept. 2006.

7. Ben Feller, "Teacher Training Is Chaotic, Study Says" *USA Today*, Sept. 18, 2006.

8. Jennifer Jordan, "State Worries Too Many Students Have Problems Reading," *Providence Journal*, Feb. 5, 2007.

9. Scores for 2004, with similar scores in 2005. Rebecca Boone, "Idaho Begins Push to Improve Teen Literacy," *Times-News Twin Falls* (Idaho), May 11, 2006.

10. Claudette Riley, "State to Unveil New Reading Strategy," *The Tennessean*, Aug. 18, 2005.

11. "Improving Adolescent Literacy," U.S. Department of Education Institute of Education Sciences report, 2007.

12. Conn Iggulden and Hal Iggulden, *The Dangerous Book for Boys* (New York: HarperCollins, 2007).

13. Dav Pilkey (Scholastic). Series started in 1998.

14. Avi, *The True Confessions of Charlotte Doyle* (New York: HarperCollins, 1990).

15. Maureen Dowd, "Heels over Hemingway," *New York Times*, Feb. 10, 2007.

16. Yvette Keel, phone interview, November 2006. I visited her middle school in 2004.

17. American Federation of Teachers, report published June 1999, http://www.aft.org/pubs-reports/downloads/teachers/rocketsci.pdf.

18. Debby Zambo and William G. Brozo, *Bright Beginnings for Boys: Engaging Young Boys in Active Literacy* (Newark, DE: International Reading Association, 2008).

19. Maria Gold, "Study Questions 'No Child' Act's Reading Plan," *Washington Post*, May 2, 2008.

20. E. D. Hirsch, *Cultural Literacy: What Every American Needs to Know* (Boston: Houghton Mifflin, 1987).

CHAPTER 4: THE WRITING FAILURES

1. *The Global Achievement Gap*, ed. Tony Wagner (New York: Basic Books, 2009).

2. "Trends in Educational Equity of Girls & Women: 2004," National Center for Education Statistics report, 2005.

3. Janet Kornblum and Greg Toppo, "Studies: SAT Writing Portion Good Predictor of Grades," *USA Today*, Apr. 24, 2008.

4. "The Neglected 'R': The Need for a Writing Revolution" (National Commission on Writing, 2003).

5. National Assessment of Educational Progress, 2002.

6. Freedman is a professor emeritus at the University of Maryland. The article is "You Can't Learn to Write Without Reading," *Education Week*, Nov. 15, 2006.

7. University of Toronto, press release, Oct. 18, 2000.

8. EdNews.org, Oct. 23, 2006.

9. Ralph Fletcher, *Boy Writers* (Portland, ME: Stenhouse, 2006).

10. Thomas Newkirk, *Misreading Masculinity: Boys, Literacy, and Popular Culture* (Portsmouth, NH: Heinemann, 2002).

11. Greg Toppo, "10 Years Later, The Real Story Behind Columbine," *USA Today*, April 14, 2009.

12. Newkirk based his observations on Malcolm Gladwell's *The Tipping Point* (Boston: Back Bay Books, 2002).

13. After six years, 55 percent of the women will graduate, compared to 40 percent of the men. Interviews with campus officials.

14. Vartan Gregorian, "Writing Next," Carnegie Corporation report, October 2006.

CHAPTER 5: THE BLAME GAME

1. Christina Hoff Sommers, *The War Against Boys: How Misguided Feminism Is Harming Our Young Men* (New York: Simon and Schuster, 2000).

2. Anick Jesdanum, "PlayStation 3 Debuts to Long Lines," *San Francisco Chronicle*, Nov. 17, 2006.

3. "Despite Large Stocks, Nintendo's WII Sells Out at Many Stores upon Launch," FOXNews.com. Nov. 20, 2006.

4. Mark Bauerlein, *The Dumbest Generation* (New York: Tarcher, 2008).

5. Elizabeth F. Farrell, "Logging On, Tuning Out," *Chronicle of Higher Education*, Sept. 2, 2005.

6. Ibid.

7. Thomas Newkirk, *Misreading Masculinity: Boys, Literacy, and Popular Culture* (Portsmouth, NH: Heinemann, 2002).

8. Lawrence Kutner and Cheryl Olson (New York: Simon and Schuster, 2008).

9. Douglas Gentile, "Pathological Video Game Use Among Youth 8 to 18: A National Study," *Psychological Science*, May 2009.

10. Donna St. George, "Study Finds Some Youths 'Addicted' to Video Games," *Washington Post*, April 20, 2009.

11. I visited Alston Middle School, Summerville, South Carolina, in August 2006.

12. Thomas Dee, "The Why Chromosome," *Education Next*, fall 2006.

13. "Black Male Teachers," editorial, *Tallahassee Democrat*, Aug. 2, 2006.

14. Jay P. Greene and Marcus A. Winters, "Leaving Boys Behind: Public High School Graduation Rates," Manhattan Institute report, April 2006.

15. "Black Male Students at Public Flagship Universities in the U.S.," Joint Center for Political and Economic Studies report, Sept. 2006.

16. *Black Males Left Behind*, ed. Ronald B. Mincy (Washington, DC: Urban Institute Press, 2006).

17. Lisa Krieger, "Colleges Recruit in Black Churches," *San Jose Mercury News*, June 12, 2006.

18. Sara Mead, "The Truth About Boys and Girls," Education Sector report, June 27, 2006.

19. Tina Kelley, "An Autism Anomaly, Partly Exposed," *New York Times*, Feb. 18, 2007.

20. http://www.nas.org.uk/nas/jsp/polopoly.jsp?d=1049&a=3370.

21. "The Extent of Drug Therapy for Attention Deficit-Hyperactivity Disorder Among Children in Public Schools," *American Journal of Public Health* (September 1999).

22. "Smart Boys Bad Grades," Learning Resources Network report, 2006.

23. "Are Boys Making the Grade?" Rennie Center for Education Research & Policy report, October 2006, renniecenter.org.

24. Michael Gurian, *The Minds of Boys* (San Francisco: Jossey-Bass, 2005).

25. Richard Whitmire, "Is Black Test-Score Gap Linked to Rap Culture? One Expert Thinks So," Gannett News Service, September 25, 1998.

26. *The Black-White Test Score Gap*, eds. Christopher Jencks and Meredith Phillips (Washington, DC: Brookings Institution Press, 1998).

27. William Pollack, *Real Boys* (New York: Henry Holt and Company, 1998).

28. Michael Kimmel, *Guyland* (New York: HarperCollins, 2008).

29. Joe Carmichiel, *Permanent Adolescence* (Far Hills, NJ: New Horizon Press, 2008).

CHAPTER 6: SOLUTIONS

1. The school has since changed to the PALS tutoring program.

2. School visits in March 2006 and April 2007.

3. Norman Bridwell, *Clifford Gets a Job* (New York: Scholastic, 1985).

4. Walter Dean Myers, *The Greatest* (New York: Scholastic, 2001).

CHAPTER 7: IMPEDIMENTS TO A SOLUTION

1. Kim Gandy, "The Patriarchy Isn't Falling," *USA Today*, Sept. 23, 2005.

2. Christina Hoff Sommers, *The War Against Boys: How Misguided Feminism Is Harming Our Young Men* (New York: Simon and Schuster, 2000).

3. Christina Hoff Sommers, *Who Stole Feminism?: How Women Betrayed Women* (New York: Simon and Schuster, 1994).

4. The most lopsided arguments denying the gender gaps arise from the American Association of University Women. See the "pushback" section of my website library at whyboysfail.com.

5. Sara Mead, "The Truth About Boys and Girls," Education Sector report, June 27, 2006.

6. In early to mid-2006 three magazine articles pointed to problems with boys: a *Newsweek* cover story, an article in *Esquire*, and an article (written by me) in *The New Republic*.

7. Wyatt Andrews, CBSNews.com, June 26, 2006.

8. Unless noted otherwise, all data are from "The State of American Manhood," Postsecondary Education Opportunity report, September 2006.

9. "Leaving Boys Behind: Public High School Graduation Rates," Manhattan Institute report, April 2006.

10. Judith Kleinfeld, "Five Powerful Strategies for Connecting Boys to School," White House Conference on Helping America's Youth, June 6, 2006.

11. Author interview, Maine Department of Labor.

12. At the end of 2005, Maine had 61,600 manufacturing jobs compared with 82,300 a decade earlier. Author interview, Maine Department of Labor.

13. Mary Madden, phone interview, December 2006.

14. "Boys in Jeopardy at School," *Portland Press Herald*, March 26, 2006.

15. On the Maine Educational Assessment, 57 percent of the girls in fourth grade and 45 percent of the boys exceeded state standards. 2003–2004 data.

16. Maine assessments, 2003–2004.

17. 2005 figures.

18. Classes entering between 1994 and 1999.

19. One exception: With its low minority population (Maine is 96 percent white), Maine's school achievement gender gap is larger than its racial achievement gap.

20. Thomas Newkirk, *Misreading Masculinity: Boys, Literacy, and Popular Culture* (Portsmouth, NH: Heinemann, 2002).

CHAPTER 8: THE INTERNATIONAL STORY

1. I visited Australia in March 2007.

2. Australian dollars. About $9,658 in American dollars.

3. *Education at a Glance: OECD Indicators*, 2006, http://dx.doi.org/10.1787/401523756323

4. On the surface Mortenson and I are at odds over the cause of the boy troubles. He emphasizes the changed job market while I lean to the literacy issue. But I see them as the same: Boys can't get tracked into the new jobs because they lack the verbal skills that are the currency of any college.

5. *Education at a Glance.*

6. Ibid.

7. Clive Kean and Ken Coates, "Snail Males: Why Are Men Falling Behind in Universities While Women Speed Ahead?" *The Walrus*, Feb. 28, 2007. Coates is the dean of arts at the University of Waterloo. Kean is director of lifelong learning at the University of Prince Edward Island.

8. Ibid.

9. "Women Learn Better, Faster," *Sunday Montreal Gazette*, Feb. 4, 2007.

10. Ibid.

11. Debbie Andalo, "Boys Closing Gender Gap in School Math and Science," *Guardian*, March 1, 2007.

12. Ibid.

CHAPTER 9: WHY THESE GENDER GAPS MATTER

1. Casey Mulligan, "A Milestone for Working Women," *New York Times*, January 14, 2009.

2. Robin Sproul, interview, October 2006.

3. Paul Farhi, "Men Signing Off; As More Women Become TV Anchors and Reporters, Males Exit the Newsroom," *Washington Post*, July 23, 2006.

4. Ibid.

5. Gumbert is chief executive of Audience Research & Development, a Fort Worth–based consulting firm.

6. Henry E. Cauvin, "Female FBI Agents Make Their Mark in Md. Amid Rise in White-Collar Crime," *Washington Post*, June 21, 2009.

7. Sam Roberts, "For Young Earners in Big City, a Gap in Women's Favor," *New York Times*, Aug. 3, 2007.

8. "No Quick Riches for New York's Twentysomethings," *Gotham Gazette*, June 2007.

9. In 2005, only 38 percent of the men in New York were college graduates, compared to 53 percent of the women. Roberts, "For Young Earners in Big City, a Gap in Women's Favor."

10. "The Gender Gap in California Higher Education," California Postsecondary Education Commission report, September 2006.

11. Mary Hegarty Nowlan, "Women Doctors, Their Ranks Growing, Transform Medicine," *Boston Globe*, Oct. 2, 2006.

12. Pam Belluck, "A New Problem for Farmers: Veterinarians in Short Supply," *New York Times*, Feb. 7, 2007.

13. Robin Wilson, "Harvard Notes a Decline in Proportion of Women Who Accepted Offers of Tenure-Track Faculty Jobs," *Chronicle of Higher Education*, Oct. 24, 2006.

14. "Gender Pay Gap in Federal Workforce Narrows," *Washington Post*, April 28, 2009.

15. Families and Work Institute, 2008.

16. Matthew Wald, "Up, Up and Never Mind," *New York Times*, Apr. 26, 2007.

17. Martha West and John Curtis, "Gender Equity Indicators 2006: Organizing Around Gender Equity," American Association of University Professors.

18. Cornelia Dean, "Women in Science: The Battle Moves to the Trenches," *New York Times,* Dec. 19, 2006.

19. Ibid.

20. "More Women on College Boards," Insidehighereducation.com, Jan. 21, 2009.

21. As of 2005 less than two-thirds of the big women's basketball programs were led by female coaches—three percentage points lower than in 2004. Only 7.8 percent of the top athletic directors' jobs are held by women at the NCAA's top level. Brad Wolverton, "Despite Small Gains, Women and Minority-Group Members Still Land Few Jobs in College Sports," *Chronicle of Higher Education,* Dec. 14, 2006.

22. Sara Lipka, "In a New Twist on 'Equal Opportunity,' a University Cuts Women's Sports," *Chronicle of Higher Education,* Nov. 3, 2006.

23. Stephanie Kassab, "JMU Students Protest Title IX Athletic Cuts," *Cavalier Daily,* Dec. 21, 2006.

24. Ibid.

25. "A Tough Time to Be a Girl: Gender Imbalances on Campus," www.whyboys fail.com, July 2008.

26. Eduardo Porter and Michelle O'Donnell, "Facing Middle Age with No Degree, and No Wife," *New York Times,* Aug. 6, 2006.

27. Ibid.

28. Between 2000 and 2005, the percentage of marriages to foreigners rose from 4 percent to 14 percent. Norimitsu Onishi, "Korean Men Use Brokers to Find Brides in Vietnam," *New York Times*, Feb. 22, 2007.

29. Ibid.

30. Sharon LaFraniere, "Chinese Bias for Baby Boys Creates a Gap of 32 Million," *New York Times,* April 10, 2009.

31. "6.3 Brides for Seven Brothers." *Economist,* Dec. 17, 1998.

32. Leonard Sax, "What's Happening to Boys?; Young Women These Days Are Driven—but Guys Lack Direction," *Washington Post,* March 31, 2006.

33. Leonard Sax, *Boys Adrift* (New York, Basic Books, 2007).

34. Emily Bazelon, "2 Kids + 0 Husband = Family," *New York Times,* Jan. 29, 2009.

CHAPTER 10: ACTIONS THAT NEED TO BE TAKEN

1. "The Gathering Storm," National Academies report, 2005.

2. Richard Garner, "Girls 13 Boys 0: Testing Reveals Gender Gap in Basic Skills," *Independent*, July 30, 2009.

3. Jon Scieszka, *The Stinky Cheese Man and Other Fairly Stupid Stories* (New York: Viking Juvenile, 1992).

4. Jon Scieszka, *The True Story of the 3 Little Pigs!* (New York: Viking Juvenile, 1999).

5. "Working Toward Excellence," *Journal of the Alabama Best Practices Center,* summer/fall 2006.

6. Jay Mathews, "Saving Young Men with Career Academies," *Washington Post,* July 21, 2008.

7. Steven Proud, "Girl Power?" Working paper, Bristol University.

8. John Sweeney, "Williamsburg County Does Away with Single Gender Education," SCNOW.com, http://www2.scnow.com/scp/business/local/article/williamsburg_county_does_away_with_single_gender_education/68389/, Aug. 7, 2009.

9. Andrew Sum, Ishwar Khatiwada, Joseph McLaughlin, "The Growing Gender Gaps in College Enrollment and Degree Attainment in the U.S. and Their Potential Economic and Social Consequences." Paper prepared for the Business Roundtable, May 2003.

10. Alex Kingsbury, "Admittedly Unequal," *U.S. News & World Report,* June 17, 2007.

11. Using the SAT scale prior to the writing exam.

12. Gadi Dechter, "Towson Angles to Draw Males; School Targets Students with Low Grades, High Test Scores," *Baltimore Sun,* Oct. 29, 2006.

13. Ibid.

14. Ibid.

15. I visited Lisby Elementary in January 2007.

16. "Schools Turn to Comics as Trial Balloon: Novel Md. Program Uses Genre to Encourage Reluctant Readers," *Washington Post,* Dec. 13, 2004.

17. Nancy Grasmick, phone interview, 2005.

18. Katherine Paterson, *Bridge to Terabithia* (New York: HarperCollins, 1977).

19. Liz Bowie, "Grasmick Urges Expanded Use of Comics in Reading," *Baltimore Sun,* May 3, 2007.

20. Elissa Gootman, "Superman Finds New Fans Among Reading Instructors," *New York Times,* Dec. 26, 2007.

21. Jamilah Evelyn, "Community Colleges Start to Ask, Where Are the Men?" *Chronicle of Higher Education,* June 28, 2002.

22. The last year the college was split evenly by gender was 1974.

APPENDIX

1. Janet Hyde and Janet Mertz, "Gender, Culture, and Mathematics Performance," Proceedings of the National Academy of Sciences, June 1, 2009.

2. U.S. Department of Education IPEDS Graduation Rate Survey (GRS) with six-year cohorts beginning in 1996, 1997, and 1998 and the Beginning Postsecondary Students Longitudinal Study (BPS), 1996–2002.

INDEX

ABOUT THE AUTHOR

Richard Whitmire, a veteran newspaper reporter and editorial writer, writes education commentaries that appear frequently in newspapers, journals, and magazines. In 2009 he was the Project Journalist for the Broad Prize for Urban Education and the writer for a New America Foundation project on developmental education in community colleges. He recently served as president of the National Education Writers Association.

After graduating from the College of Wooster in Ohio, Whitmire taught high school English and then held several newspaper jobs in upstate New York before moving to Washington to take a job handling special projects with Gannett News Service. After working on the design and launch of *USA Today* he returned to Gannett News Service to cover the Pentagon. In 1986 he received a Knight Journalism Fellowship to study national security topics at Stanford University.

After the 1991 Gulf War, Whitmire switched to reporting on education. In 2000 he joined the editorial board of *USA Today*, where he wrote editorials about education issues. In 2004 he concluded a Journalism Fellowship in Child and Family Policy at the University of Maryland, where he looked at why boys are falling behind in school. Whitmire left *USA Today* in January 2009, to begin a new career as an independent education writer.

Whitmire, who is married and has two daughters, lives in Arlington, Virginia.